# BTEC Tech Award in

# SPORT
## ACTIVITY and
# FITNESS

**Ben Hayward**
**Michael Knight**

OXFORD
UNIVERSITY PRESS

Great Clarendon Street, Oxford, OX2 6DP, United Kingdom

Oxford University Press is a department of the University of Oxford. It furthers the University's objective of excellence in research, scholarship, and education by publishing worldwide. Oxford is a registered trade mark of Oxford University Press in the UK and in certain other countries.

British Library Cataloguing in Publication Data

Data available

978-0-19-842332-4

1 3 5 7 9 10 8 6 4 2

Paper used in the production of this book is a natural, recyclable product made from wood grown in sustainable forests.

The manufacturing process conforms to the environmental regulations of the country of origin.

Printed in Great Britain by Bell and Bain Ltd. Glasgow

Oxford University Press is not responsible for content available on third-party websites. The content of these websites may have changed since publication.

OUP would like to thank Matthew Hunter, Abigail Woodman, Darren Richards, Linda McCullough, and Disability Rights UK for their help in preparing this book for publication.

# Contents

# Introduction

Welcome to your BTEC Tech Award in Sport, Activity and Fitness.

The course is divided into three components:

1. Understand the body and the supporting technology for sport and activity
2. The principles of training, nutrition, and psychology for sport and activity
3. Applying the principles of sport and activity

Each component is further divided into three learning aims.

Components 1 and 3 are assessed by assignment, and you'll be asked to complete a task at the end of each learning aim that will be marked by your teacher. Component 2 is assessed by an exam. At the end of each learning aim in this book, we've provided you with lots of guidance to help you get your head around your assignments and do well in your exam. You will also need to check in with your teacher so that you know exactly what you need to do.

When you complete each assignment you'll be awarded one of the following grades:

- Level 1 Pass
- Level 1 Merit
- Level 2 Pass
- Level 2 Merit
- Level 2 Distinction

The marking criteria for each assignment, which you'll be given as part of each task, explain exactly how you achieve each grade. The activities throughout this book will also help to prepare you for the assignments. The bronze activities will help you meet the Level 2 Pass criteria, the silver activities will help you meet the Level 2 Merit criteria, and the gold activities will help you meet the Level 2 Distinction criteria. If you push yourself to complete all the activities you'll find the assignments much easier. If you are struggling, talk to your teacher.

Enjoy the course, and good luck!

# Understand the body and the supporting technology for sport and activity

**1**

Ellie recently took part in a taster session at her local netball club. She really enjoyed the training drills and playing the adapted games, but found she got out of breath quickly and couldn't jump as high or throw the ball as hard as some of the other players. She has decided that she would like to attend the club regularly and play netball competitively, but realizes she needs to get fitter if she is going to compete for a place on the team. Having recently recovered from a sprained ankle, she also wants to learn how to minimize the risk of injury and how to recover quickly if she is unfortunate enough to hurt herself again. Technology plays an important part in fitness and injury prevention, and Ellie wants to know how it can help her achieve her goals.

This chapter will explore:

**Learning aim A: Investigate the impact of sport and activity on the body systems**

➜ 1.A1 The body systems
➜ 1.A2 The physiological impact of engagement in sport and activity on the body systems

**Learning aim B: Explore common injuries in sport and activity and methods of rehabilitation**

➜ 1.B1 Common sporting injuries
➜ 1.B2 Causes of common sporting injuries
➜ 1.B3 Management and rehabilitation of common sporting injuries

**Learning aim C: Understand the use of technology for sport and activity**

➜ 1.C Technology in sport and physical activity, and its benefits and limitations

The body is made up of a number of systems that are responsible for its effective functioning. For example, the digestive system is responsible for absorbing nutrients from our food, and the nervous system is responsible for relaying signals between our brain and our muscles.

The systems we think of most in relation to sport and physical activity are the **cardiorespiratory system**, made up of the cardiovascular system and the respiratory system, and the **musculoskeletal system**, made up of the muscular system and the skeletal system. These two systems combine to enable our bodies to move and to respond to the demands of physical activity.

## The cardiovascular system

The **cardiovascular system** is part of the cardiorespiratory system. It consists of the heart, the blood vessels (the arteries, veins, and capillaries), and the blood.

The heart is a powerful muscular pump that sends blood around the body. The heart is divided into a left side and a right side by the septum. Each side has two chambers, separated by non-return valves that prevent backflow and force the blood to travel in just one direction. The sound you can hear when you listen to your heart beat is the sound of these valves opening and closing. The top chambers are called the atria and the bottom chambers are called the ventricles.

➜ *This diagram shows how the cardiovascular system transports oxygenated and deoxygenated blood around the body.*

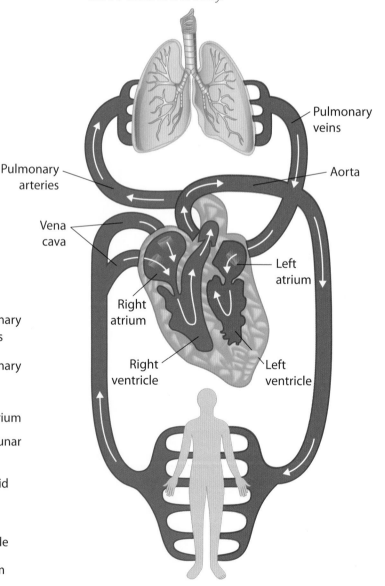

Pulmonary veins

Pulmonary arteries

Aorta

Vena cava

Left atrium

Right atrium

Right ventricle

Left ventricle

➜ *This diagram shows the structure of the heart.*

Aorta

Pulmonary arteries

Superior vena cava

Pulmonary veins

Right atrium

Left atrium

Tricuspid valve

Semi-lunar valve

Right ventricle

Bicuspid valve

Inferior vena cava

Left ventricle

Septum

The right atrium receives **deoxygenated blood** (blood containing a low concentration of oxygen) from the body through two large veins called the superior vena cava and the inferior vena cava. The deoxygenated blood is pumped from the right atrium, through the tricuspid valve and into the right ventricle, and then through a semi-lunar valve to the pulmonary arteries. The pulmonary arteries carry deoxygenated blood to the lungs, where it becomes oxygenated.

**Oxygenated blood** (blood containing a high concentration of oxygen) leaves the lungs and returns to the left atrium of the heart via the pulmonary veins. The oxygenated blood is pumped from the left atrium, through the bicuspid valve and into the left ventricle, and then through a semi-lunar valve to the aorta. The aorta, the largest artery in the body, carries the oxygenated blood to the rest of the body, where it becomes deoxygenated.

## The respiratory system

The **respiratory system** is part of the cardiorespiratory system. The structures of the respiratory system enable us to breathe.

Air is drawn into the body through the nose and mouth when we inhale (breathe in). It travels down the trachea to the bronchi ('bronchi' is the plural of 'bronchus'), down the bronchi to the bronchioles, and eventually reaches the alveoli.

When we exhale (breathe out), the air goes in the opposite direction. It starts at the alveoli, and travels up the bronchioles, up the bronchi, up the trachea, and leaves the body via the nose and mouth.

The diaphragm and the intercostals are muscles that enable us to breathe. When we breathe in, the diaphragm and intercostals contract, the space inside the lungs gets bigger, and air is pulled into the lungs. When we breathe out, the diaphragm and the intercostals relax, the space inside the lungs returns to normal, and the air inside the lungs is forced out of the body.

➜ *This diagram shows the structure of the respiratory system.*

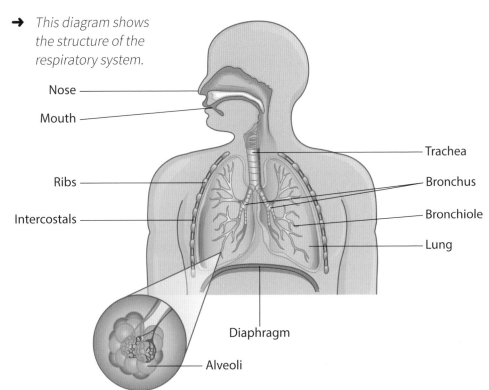

Nose

Mouth

Ribs

Intercostals

Trachea

Bronchus

Bronchiole

Lung

Diaphragm

Alveoli

**B**ronze

1. Imagine you are in a tiny submarine that can travel alongside blood cells around the cardiovascular system. Starting at the right atrium, describe your journey through the body.

**B**ronze

2. Explore your respiratory system by identifying the parts of your anatomy involved in breathing. Breathe in and out slowly and explain what you can feel. Try to use technical vocabulary in your explanation.

3. The respiratory system is often compared to an upside-down tree. Draw a diagram to illustrate this comparison. Think about the different thicknesses of branches on a tree and what you find at the end of tree branches.

# The functions of the cardiorespiratory system

The cardiorespiratory system has four main functions.

## Gaseous exchange

The cardiovascular system and the respiratory system work together to bring oxygen into the body and transport it to the working muscles and organs, and to remove the carbon dioxide created by the body when we move.

When we inhale, **oxygen intake** occurs. The air we breathe in, approximately 21 per cent of which is oxygen, travels through the respiratory system to the alveoli in the lungs.

When the alveoli fill with air, a process known as **gaseous exchange** takes place. Oxygen moves from the air in the alveoli into the blood in the capillaries. At the same time, carbon dioxide moves from the blood in the capillaries to the air in the alveoli. This happens because of a process called **diffusion**, when molecules move from an area of higher concentration to an area of lower concentration in an attempt to reach a balance.

Diffusion is possible because the capillaries, which are very small blood vessels, are wrapped tightly around the alveoli. The walls of the capillaries and the alveoli are very thin, only one cell thick, so oxygen and carbon dioxide can easily pass through them.

Once **oxygen uptake** has taken place at the alveoli, the oxygenated blood is carried to the heart and then to the working muscles and organs, where it is used to release energy. The deoxygenated blood is then carried back to the alveoli via the heart. The deoxygenated blood contains carbon dioxide, a waste product created when oxygen is used to release energy. The carbon dioxide then passes through the respiratory system and is breathed out.

Both oxygen intake and oxygen uptake increase during exercise because the working muscles demand more oxygen.

→ *This diagram shows how oxygen ($O_2$) and carbon dioxide ($CO_2$) exchange with one another in the alveoli.*

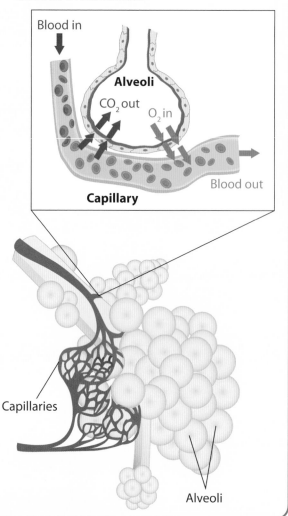

Blood in

**Alveoli**

$CO_2$ out

$O_2$ in

Blood out

**Capillary**

Capillaries

Alveoli

---

4. In pairs, decide who will take on the role of the cardiovascular system and who will take on the role of the respiratory system. Then, using your hands and any other objects that might be useful, show how the two systems work together to supply the body with oxygen and remove carbon dioxide from the body.

5. Create a video presentation (or a storyboard for one) on gaseous exchange that could be shown to a Key Stage 3 class. Consider the simplest way to explain gaseous exchange.

6. Write down all the key phrases relating to temperature regulation. Your list should include 'vasodilation', 'vasoconstriction', and 'blood vessels'. Now attempt to explain how the cardiovascular system regulates temperature without using any of these words. You'll need to be very creative! Once you've done that, write an explanation of how the cardiovascular system regulates temperature using the key phrases; you should find it much easier.

## Clotting

When the body is damaged, by a cut or other trauma, blood vessels leak blood. In response, blood flow to the damaged area is restricted. **Platelets** in the blood are activated and become sticky, grouping together over the wound to plug the hole and stop the bleeding, allowing the blood vessel to heal. This vital process is known as blood clotting.

→ *This diagram shows platelets, in pale pink, forming a clot.*

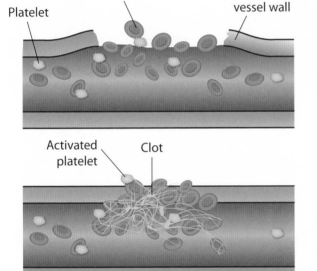

Red blood cell

Broken blood vessel wall

Platelet

Activated platelet

Clot

## Removing lactic acid

The body can release energy aerobically (with oxygen) and anaerobically (without oxygen). When energy is released anaerobically, a waste product called **lactic acid** is produced. If lactic acid builds up in our working muscles, we experience pain and fatigue. The cardiovascular system reduces the build-up of lactic acid by carrying it away from the working muscles in the blood to be broken down by the body.

When your body works at a low intensity (when you are strolling along a flat road, for example), you can work aerobically and lactic acid is not produced. When the intensity of the activity increases (when you start to walk faster because you realize you are late, for example), your body will release some of the energy required anaerobically but there is still time for oxygen to be delivered to the working muscles and for lactic acid to be carried away. However, when your body works at a high intensity (when you sprint for the bus, for example), energy will mostly be released anaerobically because oxygen cannot reach the working muscles quickly enough. Lactic acid is created and will rapidly build up if you continue sprinting.

## Temperature regulation

It is important to keep the body's internal temperature steady at 36.1–37.8°C. A significant increase in the body's internal temperature can lead to dehydration and heatstroke, while a significant decrease in the body's internal temperature can lead to hypothermia. Both can, in extreme cases, lead to death. The cardiovascular system plays an important role in temperature regulation.

During exercise, your working muscles generate heat. Blood vessels near the surface of the skin widen to allow more blood to flow towards the surface of the skin. This is called **vasodilation**. The heat generated by the muscles, carried by the blood, is then able to escape through the skin.

When you are cold, the blood vessels near the surface of the skin narrow, decreasing the volume of blood flowing towards the surface of the skin. This is called **vasoconstriction**, and it ensures that any heat generated by the body stays in the core of the body.

→ *Vasodilation*

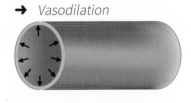

→ *Normal vascular tone*

→ *Vasoconstriction*

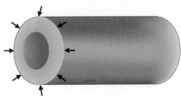

# The muscular system

The **muscular system** is part of the musculoskeletal system. There are over 650 muscles in the human body. Here are the major muscles of the muscular system:

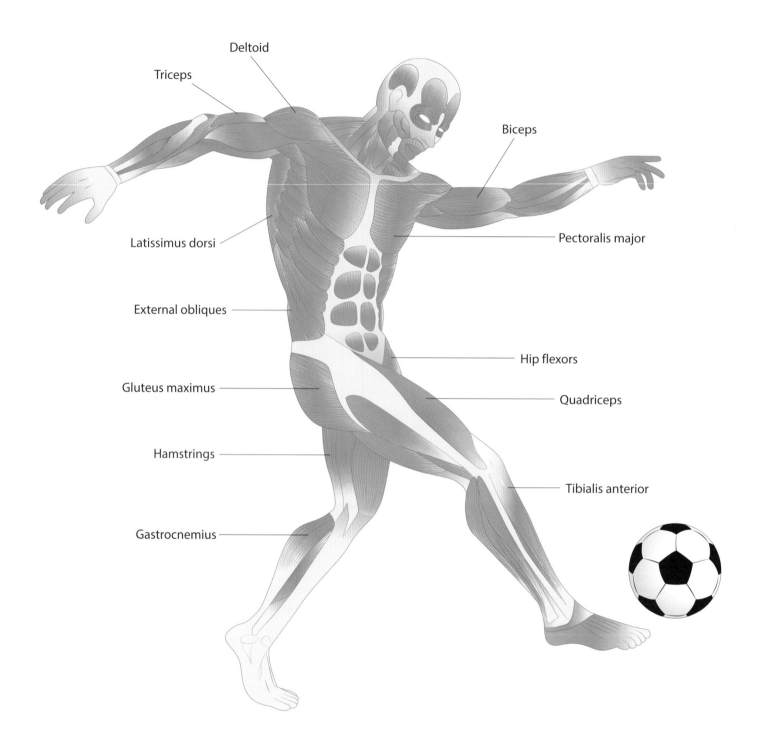

Deltoid

Triceps

Biceps

Latissimus dorsi

Pectoralis major

External obliques

Hip flexors

Gluteus maximus

Quadriceps

Hamstrings

Tibialis anterior

Gastrocnemius

# The skeletal system

The **skeletal system** is part of the musculoskeletal system. The skeleton consists of 206 bones. Here are the major bones of the skeletal system:

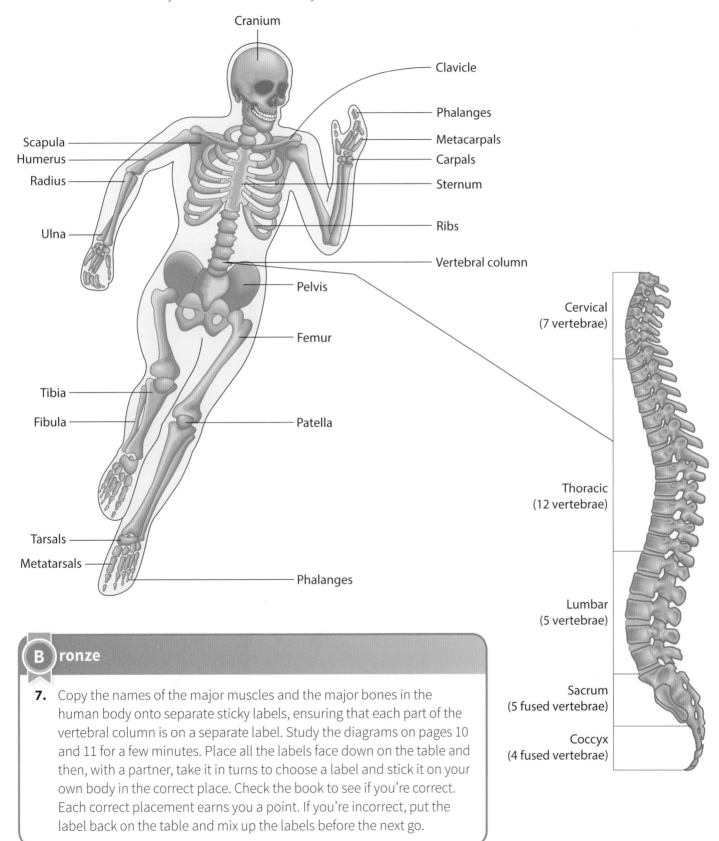

## B ronze

**7.** Copy the names of the major muscles and the major bones in the human body onto separate sticky labels, ensuring that each part of the vertebral column is on a separate label. Study the diagrams on pages 10 and 11 for a few minutes. Place all the labels face down on the table and then, with a partner, take it in turns to choose a label and stick it on your own body in the correct place. Check the book to see if you're correct. Each correct placement earns you a point. If you're incorrect, put the label back on the table and mix up the labels before the next go.

# The functions of the musculoskeletal system

The musculoskeletal system has four main functions.

## Movement

The bones of the skeletal system and the muscles of the muscular system work together to produce movement. Muscles are attached to bones via **tendons**. When a muscle contracts, the tendon transfers the effort from the muscle to the bone, the muscle pulls on the bone, and movement is achieved.

Movement takes place at joints. A **joint** is an area in the body where two or more bones meet.

For example, the biceps muscle is attached to the radius by a tendon in the forearm. When it contracts, your elbow flexes at the elbow joint.

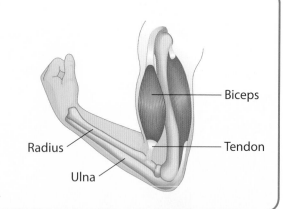

## Keeping joints stable

**Ligaments** connect bone to bone and hold a joint together, making it more stable. They are short, fibrous, and tough, so they help to prevent a joint from dislocating. A dislocation occurs when a joint is forced out of place.

For example, ligaments connect the femur to the tibia in the knee joint and help to prevent unwanted movement when a gymnast dismounts.

## Protection

The skeletal system protects vital organs. Many bones act as a rigid shell, shielding delicate organs from harm.

For example, the cranium protects the brain when heading in football, and the ribs protect the heart and lungs during a rugby tackle.

## Blood cell production

Blood cells are produced in bone marrow, which is contained in some bones. There are three main types of blood cells:

1. Red blood cells carry oxygen and other nutrients to the working muscles and organs. They also help the body remove waste products, such as carbon dioxide.
2. White blood cells fight off infections, providing immunity from disease.
3. Platelets help blood to clot following a wound.

Blood cells are carried in plasma, a watery fluid that makes blood liquid.

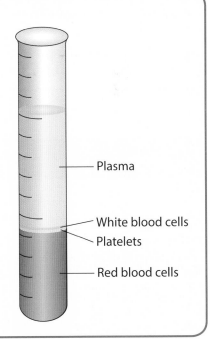

Plasma

White blood cells

Platelets

Red blood cells

➡ *This diagram shows the proportions of red blood cells, white blood cells, platelets, and plasma in blood.*

## B ronze

8. Choose a sport, then design a poster illustrating how the functions of the musculoskeletal system help a performer succeed in your chosen sport.

Regularly taking part in sport and physical activity can bring about positive **adaptations**. These long-term effects of exercise make the body systems more efficient, and mean you are better able to meet the demands of the sport or physical activity you are taking part in.

Performers will train to develop the components of fitness that are most important for their sport or physical activity, and the long-term effects of exercise on individual performers will vary as a result. However, adaptations can be divided into two broad categories: the long-term effects of exercise on the cardiorespiratory system and the long-term effects of exercise on the musculoskeletal system.

## The long-term effects of exercise on the cardiorespiratory system

### Blood becomes less viscous

Blood cells are carried in plasma, a watery fluid that makes blood liquid. When your blood does not contain a lot of plasma, it is thick and sticky; it is viscous. Viscous blood does not flow well, which means that oxygen does not reach your working muscles as quickly as it does when your blood is less viscous – when you have more plasma and your blood is runnier. Regular aerobic exercise causes your body to produce more plasma, increasing the efficiency with which oxygen is carried to your working muscles and organs and carbon dioxide is carried away from them.

**The long-term effects of exercise on the cardiorespiratory system**

### Vital capacity increases

Regular aerobic exercise increases the strength of a performer's respiratory muscles. When your diaphragm and intercostals are stronger they are better able to increase the space inside your lungs when you breathe in, pulling more air into your lungs. This increases your **vital capacity**, which is the maximum amount of air you can breathe out following a maximum breath in.

### B ronze

1. This graph shows a person's resting heart rate before and after they took part in a six-month training programme to improve their aerobic endurance. Heart rate is measured in beats per minute (bpm).

   **a)** What was the person's resting heart rate before they took part in the training programme?

   **b)** By how many beats per minute does the person's resting heart rate reduce as a result of the training programme?

   **c)** Explain why the person's resting heart rate reduces as a result of the training programme.

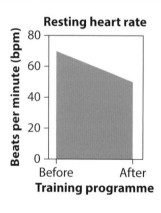

**Resting heart rate**

Beats per minute (bpm)

Before    After
**Training programme**

## Cardiac hypertrophy

As a result of regular aerobic exercise, the heart experiences **cardiac hypertrophy**. The walls of the heart become more muscular and the heart becomes more efficient. The heart can pump out more blood per beat. This results in:

- **lower resting heart rate**
  Your **heart rate** is the number of times your heart beats per minute. Your resting heart rate is the number of times your heart beats in one minute when you are at rest – in other words, when you are not exercising. An efficient heart, that pumps more blood per beat, does not need to work as hard to deliver enough blood to your muscles and organs when you are at rest, hence resting heart rate is lower with cardiac hypertrophy.

- **lower resting blood pressure**
  Your **blood pressure** is the pressure that blood leaving the heart exerts on your arteries. An efficient heart, that pumps more blood per beat, does not need to beat as powerfully to deliver enough blood to your muscles and organs when you are at rest, hence resting blood pressure is lower with cardiac hypertrophy.

## Red blood cells increase

Regular aerobic exercise causes your body to produce more red blood cells. This increases the efficiency with which oxygen is carried to your working muscles and organs, and carbon dioxide is carried away from them.

## Gaseous exchange becomes more efficient

Gaseous exchange is the process by which oxygen moves from the air we breathe in into our blood and carbon dioxide moves from our blood into the air we breathe out. Gaseous exchange takes place at the alveoli in the lungs. Regular aerobic exercise increases the number of capillaries wrapped around the alveoli, which means that more gaseous exchange takes place. As a result, the speed at which oxygen, is delivered and carbon dioxide is removed increases.

### S ilver

2. **a)** Read George's story and methodically examine the changes that will have occurred to his cardiorespiratory system as a result of his long-term commitment to parkrun. Explain how regular aerobic exercise caused each adaptation. You will need to carry out some research, using other textbooks or the internet, to develop a detailed understanding of each adaptation.

   > George is 47 years old. Six months ago, he went along to his local park and took part in his first parkrun. He has been returning each week ever since. His first 5K took him nearly an hour to complete, as he had to walk quite a bit, but he is now running the distance in 31 minutes. He has lost 5kg and has much more energy.

   **b)** Prepare a presentation to share your findings.

# The long-term effects of exercise on the musculoskeletal system

## Hypertrophy

Taking part in regular strength training stresses your muscles. The tension, fatigue, and damage caused prompt the muscle fibres to grow larger and stronger. This process is called **hypertrophy**.

Your core muscles are the muscles that maintain stability around your lower back, pelvis, and abdomen. Your abdominal muscles (including your rectus abdominis, your internal obliques, and your external obliques) combine with the muscles in your lower back to help support the area and prevent unwanted movement. In this way, a strong core creates a stable base that allows you to perform powerful athletic movements with the rest of your body. Your core muscles benefit from hypertrophy during strength training, just like the muscles in your arms and legs.

→ *Matt Ritchie of Newcastle United is working on strengthening his quadriceps and gluteus maximus muscles. In the process, he is contracting his core muscles to provide the stability needed to lift the weight and the core muscles become stronger as a result.*

→ *Kelly Gallagher, a ski racer, is focusing on strengthening her core muscles specifically, by performing a side plank.*

## The long-term effects of exercise on the musculoskeletal system

### Bone density increases
Performing regular load-bearing exercises stresses your bones and joints. In response, **bone density** increases to protect you from bone fractures. Calcium is deposited on the bones and they become thicker and stronger as a result.

### Tendons and ligaments become stronger
Taking part in regular strength training places your ligaments and tendons under stress. In response, their fibres thicken and become stronger and more resilient. Tendons and ligaments take a lot longer than muscles to become stronger.

**S ilver**

3. **a)** Read Becky and Linda's story and methodically examine the changes that will occur to their musculoskeletal systems if they visit the gym regularly over the long term. Explain how regular exercise will cause each adaptation. You will need to carry out some research, using other textbooks or the internet, to develop a detailed understanding of each adaptation.

> Becky is 18 and her mum, Linda, is 56. They have just joined a gym. Becky is a keen basketball player who has been playing for her county in the under-18s squad and wants to improve her strength so she will be selected for the adult squad. Linda has been encouraged to do strength training by her GP, as a recent bone density scan revealed her bone mineral levels are slightly below normal.

**b)** Prepare a presentation to share your findings.

## The effect of regular participation on a participant's components of fitness

*Regular* aerobic exercise will, over time, bring adaptations to the cardiorespiratory system. Together these adaptations can improve a performer's aerobic endurance and body composition. You will find out more about these components of fitness in Component 2 (see pages 52 and 58).

*Regular* exercise will, over time, also bring adaptations to the musculoskeletal system. Together these adaptations can improve a performer's muscular endurance, strength, and body composition. You will find out more about these components of fitness in Component 2 (see pages 53, 56 and 58).

**G**old

**4.** Read the following case studies and complete the activities below.

**Tirunesh Dibaba is a long-distance runner.**

Long-distance runners need good aerobic endurance. Their bodies need to deliver oxygenated blood to their working muscles and remove waste products, such as carbon dioxide and lactic acid, quickly so that they can keep running over long distances.

Long-distance runners also need good muscular endurance. They need to be able to move their bodies for a long period of time, contracting their muscles powerfully, repeatedly, and without fatigue.

**Jack Oliver is a weightlifter.**

Weightlifters need good muscular strength. Their bodies need to be able to generate a large force to overcome the resistance of the weight they are lifting.

**a)** Look back at the adaptations to the cardiorespiratory system and the musculoskeletal system that result from long-term participation in sport and physical activity. Which adaptations would benefit Tirunesh, which adaptations would benefit Jack, and which adaptations would benefit them both? Use a Venn diagram, like the one shown, to record your ideas.

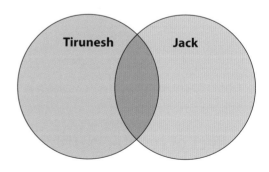

**b)** Evaluate the extent to which Tirunesh or Jack benefits from the adaptations to the cardiorespiratory and musculoskeletal systems brought about by long-term involvement in sport and physical activity.

When you are asked to evaluate something, you need to bring together all the information you have about the topic and review it before reaching a conclusion. In this case, you should weigh up the relative importance of each adaptation to Tirunesh or Jack's success in their chosen sport and come to a conclusion about which adaptation benefits them most.

**Learning aim A:** Investigate the impact of sport and activity on the body systems

## Scenario

As someone who enjoys taking part in sport and physical activity, it is important to understand how your cardiorespiratory and musculoskeletal systems work. Understanding the long-term effects of exercise on your body can also help you develop the appropriate components of fitness for success in your chosen sport. You have been asked, by your coach, to prepare a presentation for the other members of your club on the impact of sport and activity on the body systems.

## Task

Prepare a presentation, accompanied by detailed supporting notes, that shows how the cardiorespiratory and musculoskeletal systems work, how regular participation leads to adaptations, and how different sports activities benefit from different adaptations. You should:

**Level 1 PASS**
→ Identify the structures of the muscular, skeletal, respiratory, and cardiovascular systems (A.1P1).
→ Identify some of the long-term adaptations to body systems caused by regular participation in sport and activity (A.1P2).

**Level 1 MERIT**
→ Outline the structures and functions of the musculoskeletal and cardiorespiratory systems (A.1M1).
→ Outline some of the long-term adaptations to body systems caused by regular participation in sport and activity (A.1M2).

**Level 2 PASS**
→ Explain the structure and functions of the muscular, skeletal, respiratory, and cardiovascular systems (A.2P1).
→ Explain the long-term adaptations to body systems caused by regular participation in sport and activity (A.2P2).

**Level 2 MERIT**
→ Analyse how regular sports participation leads to long-term physical benefits in the body systems (A.2M1).

**Level 2 DISTINCTION**
→ Evaluate the extent to which different sports activities benefit from adaptations to the musculoskeletal and cardiorespiratory systems (A.2D1).

## Tackling the assignment

Begin your presentation by explaining the structure and functions of the four body systems and the adaptations that occur as a result of regular participation in sport and physical activity. When you <u>explain</u> something, you need to provide examples or evidence to illustrate your description or provide reasons to tell the reader why it is like it is.

Next, you must make sure that your presentation makes a clear link between the adaptations that you have explained and the benefits these adaptations bring to performers. Remember to present your ideas in a logical order, working through each detailed point you want to make methodically. This is your <u>analysis</u>.

Finally, compare and contrast the benefits of the adaptations for different sports. You will need to consider at least two very different sports. Remember, when you <u>evaluate</u> something, you need to bring together all the information you have about a topic and review it before reaching a conclusion.

## Meeting the **Level 2 Pass** criteria

### The long-term adaptations to the cardiorespiratory system: Notes to accompany my presentation

The long-term effects of regular participation in sport and physical activity on the cardiorespiratory system help its ability to deliver oxygen to working muscles.

Taking part in sport and physical activity encourages the heart to enlarge as a result of cardiac hypertrophy. Cardiac hypertrophy means more blood can be pumped with each beat as the walls of the heart thicken and get stronger. The increase in the volume of blood pumped with each beat of the heart leads to a drop in resting heart rate and means we have a lower heart rate when exercising, making exercise feel easier.

The learner has clearly explained one adaptation to the cardiovascular system – cardiac hypertrophy – and the impact it has on resting heart rate and exercising heart rate.

If the learner has already explained the four body systems and continues to explain the adaptations like this, including appropriate examples to illustrate each adaptation, they should meet the Level 2 Pass criteria.

## Meeting the Level 2 Merit criteria

### The long-term benefits of regular participation in sport and physical activity: Notes to accompany my presentation

Regular participation in sport and physical activity can lead to many long-term physical benefits to the human body.

#### Cardiac hypertrophy

Regular aerobic exercise causes the heart to grow in size. This phenomenon is known as cardiac hypertrophy. It means the heart can pump more blood with each beat, leading to a lower resting heart rate and lower resting blood pressure. The average resting heart rate is around 70 beats per minute, but trained athletes often have resting heart rates below 50 beats per minute.

Cardiac hypertrophy also means that the heart is able to pump more blood with each beat when the body is exercising at a high intensity. The adaptation leads, therefore, to an improvement in a performer's aerobic endurance. A performer with cardiac hypertrophy can perform for longer aerobically at a higher intensity, because their heart is able to help deliver more oxygenated blood to their working muscles and remove more waste products, such as carbon dioxide and lactic acid, with each beat.

> In the first section, the learner has clearly explained one adaptation to the cardiovascular system – cardiac hypertrophy – and the impact it has on resting heart rate and resting blood pressure, but they have also gone a step further by making a link between regular aerobic exercise and cardiac hypertrophy. They have also discussed how the adaptation benefits a sports performer.

> If the learner has already explained the four body systems and continues analysing the long-term benefits of regular participation like this, they should meet the Level 2 Merit criteria.

## Meeting the Level 2 Distinction criteria

### Notes to accompany my presentation (continued)

#### The benefits of cardiac hypertrophy

Cardiac hypertrophy benefits many sports performers. The increase in the volume of blood pumped out by the heart each time it beats, means that more oxygenated blood is delivered to the working muscles. This benefits a long-distance cyclist because they will be able to work aerobically at a higher intensity for longer. Their aerobic endurance will improve, and it will take longer before they experience a painful build-up of lactic acid and become fatigued.

Cardiac hypertrophy also benefits a squash player. Squash involves periods of intense work, when energy is delivered to the working muscles anaerobically, and periods of less intense work, when the lactic acid produced while the performer is working anaerobically needs to be removed. An increase in the volume of oxygen delivered to the working muscles speeds up the time it takes for the cardiovascular system to carry the lactic acid away from the working muscles. This allows the squash player to play for longer before they experience a painful build-up of lactic acid and become fatigued.

> This learner is comparing and contrasting the benefits of cardiac hypertrophy for two very different sports performers, a long-distance cyclist and a squash player. This demonstrates a comprehensive understanding of cardiac hypertrophy.

> If the learner continues to discuss the other adaptations in the same way, they should meet the Level 2 Distinction criteria provided they have already met the Level 2 Pass and Merit criteria.

Injuries are not inevitable, but it is very rare for someone involved in sport and physical activity to remain injury-free throughout their life. It is, therefore, sensible to have an awareness of some of the injuries you, or the people in the activity sessions you are leading, may experience. Having an awareness of what may happen will ensure you are better prepared to respond to an injury if something does happen, and more conscious of what you can do as a participant and as a leader to prevent injuries happening in the first place.

Warming up before you take part in sport and physical activity and cooling down afterwards can help you avoid injury. This is because a warm-up prepares your mind and body for the work ahead, and a cool-down brings your heart rate and breathing rate back to their resting rates and helps to remove the lactic acid that has built up in your working muscles during the main activity. So always make sure you take the time to do a proper warm-up and cool-down!

### Link

You can find out about the components of a warm-up and a cool-down on pages 137 and 140.

The first, and probably the most important, thing to remember when it comes to injuries is that you should stop if you feel pain. Pain is your body's way of telling you that what you are doing is causing damage. Failing to listen to the warning can make injuries worse and delay recovery.

## Common basic sporting injuries

### Sprain

A **sprain** happens when a ligament (the connective tissue that connects bone to bone and holds a joint together to make it more stable) twists beyond its normal range.

The main symptom of a sprain is pain, which you will feel immediately and which will get worse. If the sprain is severe, you will also experience some swelling, the site of the injury will feel hot, and you will be unable to move the joint normally. Later, when the swelling dies down, you may experience bruising and the joint will feel tender to the touch and weak.

→ *Simona Halep of Romania receives treatment during a tennis match at Wimbledon.*

## Strain

A **strain** happens when a muscle or tendon (the connective tissue that connects muscle to bone) is stretched beyond its normal range.

The symptoms of a strain include pain when the affected muscle (or the muscle the affected tendon is attached to) contracts, swelling, redness, weakness, and loss of function. Pain may also be felt when the affected muscle (or the muscle the affected tendon is attached to) is at rest.

## Bruise

A **bruise** is caused when blood vessels (capillaries) rupture and bleed beneath the skin as a result of a direct blow or other trauma.

The symptoms of a bruise close to the skin are pain, tenderness (the area feels painful when touched), and discolouration. If the bruise happens deep inside your body, your skin will not change colour but you may be able to feel pain and swelling.

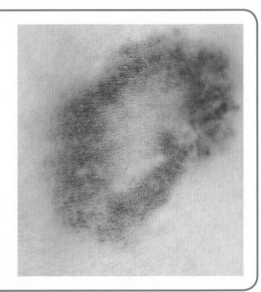

### Bronze/Silver

1.  **a)** Find out about two sports performers, one who has recently suffered a sprain and one who has recently suffered a strain. Which parts of their bodies did they injure and how did the injuries happen?

    **b)** Use the information you have collected to provide examples or evidence to explain the difference between a sprain and a strain.

### Bronze

2.  Create a meme to remind people that warming up and cooling down properly can reduce their risk of injury or to remind people that they should stop what they are doing if it is causing them pain.

# Common complex sporting injuries

## Dislocation

A **dislocation** happens when the bones at a joint are displaced, when a bone 'pops' out of place as a result of a blow or a fall. For example, catching a ball can cause a finger to dislocate and a fall can cause the shoulder to dislocate.

The symptoms of a dislocation include intense pain, difficulty in moving the joint, and, usually, an obvious deformity. The affected limb will feel numb, and this loss of sensation may also be accompanied by tingling. The joint can also swell quite quickly and become discoloured as surrounding blood vessels and ligaments are also damaged.

→ *Mark Hanretty dislocates his shoulder during* Dancing on Ice.

## Fracture

A **fracture** is a broken bone. There are three types of fracture:

- stress fractures, when tiny cracks appear in the bone; a stress fracture is often caused by repeated impact and is, therefore, referred to as an overuse injury
- open fractures, when the bone pierces the skin
- closed fractures, when the bone does not pierce the skin.

The symptoms of a fracture include pain and swelling or bruising where the fracture has occurred. You will be able to see the bone poking through the skin with an open fracture, and both open and closed fractures result in deformity and loss of function. If open and closed fractures occur in the lower limbs, the limbs will not bear your weight and you will find it difficult to stand up.

→ *Long-distance runners are more likely to suffer from stress fractures to the femur, tibia, fibula, and metatarsals than other sports performers. This is because the bones in their legs and feet experience repeated impacts as they cover long distances in training and competition.*

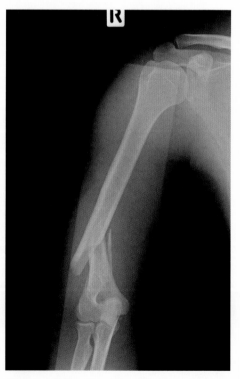

→ *An X-ray of a closed fracture.*

## Torn ligament

A ligament connects bone to bone and holds a joint together, making it more stable. Ligaments can tear when stretched beyond their normal range of movement.

Symptoms of a **torn ligament** include immediate swelling and the joint feeling warmer to the touch. The joint will feel unstable and it will be painful to move it. You might also hear a popping noise when the ligament tears.

➔ *Aliya Mustafina of Russia tears a ligament in her knee.*

## Shin splints

**Shin splints** can occur with overuse, particularly after running on hard surfaces.

The main symptom of shin splints is an aching pain on the inside of the lower leg, in the shins. It is often experienced first thing in the morning, getting worse when exercising and better when resting. The pain is often accompanied by numbness in the feet and slight swelling.

➔ *Phil Jones suffered from shin splints in 2014, keeping him off the pitch for over three months.*

## Tendonitis

**Tendonitis** occurs when tendons, which connect muscle to bone, become inflamed at a joint. Tendonitis can be, but is not always, an overuse injury.

The symptoms of tendonitis include acute pain and stiffness, which tend to be at their worst first thing in the morning, get better during the day as you move around, and then reappear towards the end of the day when you are tired. The affected tendon may be tender (painful when it is touched), especially when the associated muscle is contracting, and it may also be warm.

➔ *Tennis elbow is tendonitis that occurs at the elbow. It is caused by overusing the muscles and tendons that are attached to your elbow and used to straighten your wrist. It is sometimes, but not always, caused by playing tennis.*

### B ronze

3. Describe a complex sporting injury that you have witnessed or experienced personally or have seen happen on the television or on the internet. What caused the injury? What symptoms were experienced? How was the injury treated? And what, if anything, could have been done to avoid the injury?

Understanding the causes of common sporting injuries and how they can be prevented helps a sports leader do everything they can to keep participants safe and healthy.

The causes of common sporting injuries can be divided into categories.

## Physiological causes of common sporting injuries

- **Working at an inappropriate intensity, or doing too much too soon, can lead to injury.** Often, when embarking on a new exercise programme or taking up a new sport, participants rush to push their bodies as far as they can straightaway, and they end up injuring themselves because they haven't given themselves time to adapt to the demands of the activity. Applying the FITT principles – thinking carefully about the Frequency, Intensity, Type, and Time of the activities that you take part in – can help you work at an appropriate intensity.

- Gravity is the force that pulls things, including the human body, towards the ground. **Gravity makes balancing and landing after a jump or a somersault particularly difficult.** If a foot is placed incorrectly on landing or the opposing force provided by your muscles is not greater than the force of gravity, you will fall to the ground and can hurt yourself. It is, therefore, important to build up to performing complex skills, such as a somersault, using equipment to help you develop a safe technique.

- **Some sports are inherently more dangerous than others.** For example, people who take part in contact sports, such as football, are more likely to pick up injuries than people who take part in non-contact sports such as netball; all it takes is one mistimed tackle. However, following the rules and regulations of the sport, listening to officials, and wearing appropriate personal protective equipment can minimize the risk in taking part.

## Psychological causes of common sporting injuries

- **Low self-confidence, not believing that you can do something and being tentative when challenging opponents, can result in injury.** For example, if you decide to tackle your opponent in rugby but do not throw yourself into the tackle because you think it will fail, then you are more likely to approach your opponent in a way that leaves you vulnerable to being overpowered and hurt. It is, therefore, important to build your confidence through a structured training or coaching programme before performing potentially dangerous skills, and to believe in your own ability. This is especially important when returning to sport or physical activity after an injury, when your self-confidence is particularly low.

**B ronze**

1.  Discuss whether experienced or inexperienced performers are more likely to suffer from injuries caused by working at an inappropriate intensity.

- **Peer pressure can push you into doing something you are not ready to do, and this can lead to injury.** For example, your friends might urge you to perform a dismount in gymnastics that you have not practised and which is beyond your ability level. If you try it, you could land badly and seriously hurt yourself. So it is important to know your limits, to know what you can and cannot do. To succeed, you must push yourself, but not beyond what you can do safely.
- When you are stressed your body releases chemicals that make it hard to concentrate. **A lack of concentration can lead to trips, falls, and other mistakes, which can result in injury.** The more dangerous an activity is, the greater the effects of poor concentration. Managing stress and anxiety is important in all aspects of your life, but it is particularly important when you are performing complex physical skills.

## Environmental causes of common sporting injuries

- **Bad weather, particularly rain and high winds, can make playing surfaces dangerous.** For example, rain can lead to flooding and muddy pitches, increasing the risk of slipping and falling and, consequently, the risk of injury. Before taking part in sport and physical activity outdoors, it is important to consider the weather and respond accordingly. If the weather is particularly bad, can you move indoors or change what you are planning to do, to minimize the risks to participants?
- **It is important for participants to stay warm and dry during cold weather, to warm up properly, and to keep moving throughout an activity session.** Cold muscles do not move or stretch as well as warm muscles, increasing the risk of strains. Also, if your body temperature drops very quickly, from its normal temperature of 37 degrees Celsius to below 35 degrees Celsius, you can experience hypothermia, which can be very serious if not treated quickly.
- **It is also important to keep cool in hot weather, staying out of the sun and drinking lots of fluids to keep hydrated.** This is because it is harder for the body to cool itself in hot weather, which can lead to heatstroke and heat exhaustion. You are also at risk of sunburn, so it is vital to wear suntan lotion in very hot and sunny weather.

**B** ronze

2. Discuss situations in which peer pressure can push a person to do something they are not ready to do in the context of sport and physical activity. How would you advise a person in these situations to respond?

**S** ilver

3. Find out about hyperthermia. Explain what it is and how you can avoid it while taking part in sport and physical activity.

## Equipment-related causes of common sporting injuries

- **Wearing the wrong clothing and footwear, or clothing and footwear that do not fit properly, can dramatically increase your risk of injury in many sports.** For example, wearing trainers rather than hiking boots on a fell walk can increase your risk of slipping and falling or spraining your ankle. Always wear appropriate clothing and footwear.

- **Failing to wear the correct protective clothing or failing to use the correct protective equipment can make you vulnerable to injury.** For example, in football, shin pads protect the tibia, which can receive significant kicks and blows during tackles, from injury. Always wear mandatory protective clothing and carefully consider wearing protective clothing that is only optional.

- **Faulty or damaged equipment can seriously injure participants or other people nearby.** For example, if the springs that attach the bed of a trampoline to the outer padding are not properly attached, participants can fall through the gaps and scrape themselves on the detached springs. Always check your equipment and do not use it if it is faulty or damaged.

- **Using equipment incorrectly can cause injuries.** For example, using free weights with poor technique or lifting weights that are too heavy for you can result in strains, torn ligaments, and even dislocations. Always make sure that you know how to use equipment correctly and how to perform skills safely.

## People-related causes of common sporting injuries

- **The rules and regulations of most sports prevent young performers playing outside of their age category.** In contact and combat sports like rugby league, rugby union, and boxing, these rules are especially important to ensure that young people are not placed in high-risk situations. In many contact sports, boys and girls are only permitted to train and compete in mixed groups until around the start of puberty, when some boys grow quickly and develop a more muscular build than girls of the same age. It is therefore important to take part in sport and physical activity that is appropriate for your age and body.

- **Drinking alcohol and taking recreational drugs can reduce your ability to concentrate and react quickly, can mask the pain that is telling you to stop, and can make you more aggressive and unpredictable.** This can put you and others in danger. It is advisable neither to drink alcohol to excess nor to take recreational drugs, but never drink alcohol or take recreational drugs before taking part in sport and physical activity.

- **Participants with a low skill level and a lack of experience often suffer from injuries because they try to do something they are not capable of doing.** For example, a large proportion of injuries to skiers occur because participants lose control when skiing on terrain that is beyond their skill level. Having a low skill level and lack of experience does not, in itself, lead to injury. It is a low skill level and lack of experience coupled with overconfidence that leads to injury. So know your limits!

- **Failing to warm up properly puts you at greater risk of injury.** A warm-up should increase your heart rate and get your blood flowing around your body more quickly, it should mobilize your joints so that they can move at

**S** ilver

4. Research the protective clothing and equipment used in a sport of your choice. Then write no more than 150 words explaining how it reduces the risk of participants suffering from an injury while taking part in that sport.

their full range of movement, and it should stretch your muscles to prepare them for the activity ahead. Always warm up before sport or physical activity.

- **Overtraining – doing too much or not allowing adequate periods of rest between training sessions – can lead to overuse injuries.** Overuse injuries can be avoided by applying the FITT principles, thinking carefully about the Frequency, Intensity, Type, and Time of the activities that you take part in. Listen to your body; if you really are too tired to exercise, take a break.

## Coaching-related causes of common sporting injuries

- **A coach who employs poor training methods puts participants at risk of injury.** For example, asking participants to perform exercises that received wisdom now believes are dangerous or failing to give participants the opportunity to warm up or cool down adequately puts participants at risk. While it is important to respect your coach and follow their advice, it is also important to have the self-confidence to speak to a coach who is asking you to do things that you do not feel are appropriate.

- **A coach who encourages unsafe practices may cause harm to the participants in their care.** For example, a junior coach who does not separate players by age will be responsible for any injuries experienced by younger, smaller children who are overpowered by older, larger children. Knowing the rules and regulations of the sport or physical activity you are taking part in, and having an understanding of the causes of common sporting injuries, will enable you to identify unsafe practices so that you can discuss them with the coach.

- **A coach who teaches poor technique, or who does not correct poor technique, will be responsible for any injuries participants suffer as a result.** For example, a coach who is teaching the side tackle in rugby needs to ensure the tackler's head is positioned behind the opponent's thigh to reduce the risk of head injuries. If you are working with a coach who teaches poor technique, you would be advised to find another coach.

- **Inexperienced coaches may fail to spot dangerous situations occurring.** This is why it is important for all inexperienced coaches to be supported by a senior coach, who can monitor what is happening and help their more inexperienced colleague modify what they are doing if necessary.

**S**ilver

5. Research either rugby or basketball and explain how the rules, equipment, and scoring are adapted for children aged 8–10.

**B**ronze

6. If can be difficult to raise a concern about what a person in authority is doing, but practising difficult conversations can give you the self-confidence you need to tackle the problem. Discuss how you would react in the following situation if the coach was inexperienced and if the coach was experienced:

> A gymnastics coach you have been working with for some time likes to end coaching sessions with younger gymnasts by performing more advanced moves, such as front flips, and encouraging the children to copy. You get on well with this coach, who has really helped you progress, and you want to keep working with them, but you are worried that some of the children may be injured because they are being encouraged to perform moves that they are not ready for.

Sometimes, despite the best efforts of the sports leader, a participant will get injured. It is, therefore, important to understand what to do immediately after an accident and how you can help the participant return to full fitness so they can continue taking part in sport and physical activity. Technology has an important role to play in this process.

## First aid

**SALTAPS** describes the steps that should be taken to assess an injury.

You must follow the steps in order and you must not move on to the next step until both you and the injured participant are satisfied that the current step has been fully completed. For example, you should not touch the area until you have looked at it first and are happy that it looks alright to touch.

 With the exception of 'stop play', all the steps must be carried out by an appropriately qualified first aider.

SALTAPS is not an alternative to seeking medical advice, and if at any point you are unable to move on to the next stage, then you should seek urgent medical attention from a doctor, either by calling for an ambulance or by taking the injured participant to Accident and Emergency at the nearest hospital.

**S**top play
The first step is to stop play, so that other participants are safe and so that attention can be given to the injured participant.

**A**sk
Check how the participant feels. It is useful to ask them to rate the level of pain they are experiencing on a scale of 1 to 10 (1 = no pain; 10 = severe pain), to give you an indication of how serious the injury could be. However, it is important to remember that, in situations where they do not feel any pain, this does not mean the injury is not severe. Shock may mean that the participant does not feel pain until later on.

**L**ook
Check the injured area to see how serious the injury could be. But remember, just because something looks like a minor injury, does not mean that it is.

**T**ouch
Touch the affected area if the participant will allow you to. Be very gentle. If a leg or an arm is fractured, it is sometimes possible to feel the fracture. Ask the participant if they can feel your touch. If they cannot feel you touching them, then the injury is likely to be serious.

**A**ctive movement
Ask the participant to move the affected limb. For example, if it is a leg injury, ask them if they can move their toes and feet first and then ask them if they can move their whole leg.

**P**assive movement
If the participant cannot move the affected limb on their own, ask them if you can move it for them. Does moving it increase the pain? Is there sufficient range of movement at the joint?

**S**tand up
If all other steps are completed to both your satisfaction and the participant's, then the last step is to ask the participant to stand up. This is particularly the case if it is the leg or foot that is injured. You may need to support the participant's body weight as they get up. Sometimes this step will show how serious the injury actually is, because putting weight on an injured area will often cause extreme pain and a participant may be in denial about the extent of the injury until they try to put weight on it.

Sprains and strains can be treated immediately by a first aider using the **PRICE** method.

**P**rotect
Prevent further injury occurring by protecting the injured area.

**R**est
Rest the injured area.

**I**ce
Apply an ice pack to the affected area.

**C**ompression
Apply gentle but substantial compression to the injury.

**E**levation
Raise the injured body part above the level of the heart.

If, after a few days, there has been little or no improvement, the injured person should seek professional medical help. They should visit their GP if the injury fails to improve with self-care or the swelling gets worse. If the injury takes longer to heal than expected, the injured person could consult a physiotherapist who will be able to provide treatment and guidance.

➔ *Watch any football match and you will see the medical team work through the SALTAPS steps when they come onto the pitch to help an injured player.*

**B**ronze

1. Work with a partner to role-play the scenarios below. Take it in turns to be the casualty.

   **a)** A teammate collapses after colliding with an opponent during a game of rugby. His leg hurts very badly and he cannot stand up. Demonstrate how SALTAPS helps you deal with the situation.

   **b)** You are playing basketball at lunchtime and your friend sprains his ankle. Demonstrate how PRICE helps you deal with the situation.

# Basic rehabilitation techniques

**Rehabilitation** is the process of restoring someone to full health after any injury. Rehabilitation techniques can be grouped into physiological techniques, which focus on returning the body to full health, and psychological techniques, which focus on helping the injured person stay positive, focused, and calm throughout the healing process. Several techniques will usually be blended into a rehabilitation plan to help a performer recover from an injury.

## Ice baths

Ice baths cool the body. The blood vessels near the surface of the skin undergo vasoconstriction. This means they narrow, decreasing the volume of blood flowing to the surface of the skin, limiting the bruising caused when capillaries rupture and bleed beneath the skin, and reducing the swelling caused by sprains and strains.

## Hot and cold treatment

Alternating between an ice pack and a heat pack stimulates the blood flow to the injured area. Blood flow increases as the area heats up and decreases as the area cools. Stimulating the blood flow improves the delivery of endorphins (reducing your perception of pain and triggering a positive feeling), white blood cells (to fight off infection), and red blood cells (which carry oxygen to aid the healing process) to the site of the injury.

Hot and cold treatment reduces stiffness and soreness. It also decreases the likelihood of muscle spasms, which cause the muscle to contract and can make an injury worse.

Hot and cold treatment can be used in the treatment of sprains and strains after the initial swelling has died down.

## Physiological rehabilitation techniques

## Strapping

Strappings restrict the amount of movement possible at the affected area. For example, using a tubigrip strapping on an ankle injury prevents the ankle moving through its full range of movement, reducing the stress on the muscles, ligaments, and tendons, and helping to reduce recovery time.

## Flexibility exercises, yoga, and Pilates

Yoga involves performing a series of postures while focusing on your breathing. It increases strength and flexibility, and helps bring the mind and the body together. Pilates is an exercise system designed to improve strength, particularly core strength, and flexibility.

Like more general flexibility exercises, yoga and Pilates can be helpful during rehabilitation. They can help damaged joints regain their full range of movement and increase the strength and flexibility of damaged muscles, ligaments, and tendons. They also allow participants to keep exercising gently while they are recovering from a serious injury, because they can be modified to limit the impact on the damaged area.

## Time

Rehabilitation takes time. Some injuries will take longer than others to get better, with fractures taking a lot longer to mend than sprains and strains, for example, but all injuries need time to heal. It is, therefore, of the utmost importance that you do not return to sport and physical activity too soon after an injury and that you follow the guidance you are given by medical professionals. Returning too soon can make an injury worse and, ultimately, increase overall recovery time.

## Psychological rehabilitation techniques

## Goal setting

The principle of reversibility means that fitness gains are lost relatively quickly when training stops or reduces, as it must when you are injured. This can be very demoralizing. However, staying positive throughout the rehabilitation process is known to aid recovery. Setting goals can encourage an injured participant to take an active role in their recovery, to focus on the small improvements they are making towards full recovery, and to keep positive and motivated throughout.

### 🔗 Link

Setting SMART targets helps ensure goals are as motivating as possible. You can find out about SMART targets on page 109.

## Relaxation techniques

Relaxing the mind effectively can aid recovery because it prevents frustration, impatience, and anger building up, and can stop the downward spiral into depression. There are many different relaxation techniques, including mind-to-muscle relaxation and visualization.

Visualization involves finding a quiet place to sit or lie comfortably and imagining yourself performing successfully and without injury: imagining yourself running hard, jumping high, performing the perfect dismount, or hitting the perfect serve. Studies have suggested that visualizing the healing process and the healed body performing can actually aid the recovery process and slow down reversibility, as your mind and body work together to overcome the injury.

### 🏅 Silver

2. Imagine that you have sprained your ankle playing tennis. Explain the physiological and psychological rehabilitation techniques you might use to aid your recovery.

# The use of technology in rehabilitation

As in all areas of life, technology has brought new techniques for rehabilitation. Here we look at four of them: whole-body cryotherapy, hyperbaric oxygen treatment, resistance bands, and electronic pulse massage systems.

## Whole-body cryotherapy

Whole-body cryotherapy is said to improve the time it takes performers to recover from injuries and reduce the likelihood that they will get injured in the first place. It is a technologically advanced – and colder – version of the ice pack or the ice bath.

First you enter a pre-chamber for about one minute, where the temperature is −65 to −70 degrees Celsius. When you are acclimatized, you move into the main chamber, where the temperature is as low as −135 degrees Celsius, for a further two minutes.

> '*It helps recovery and rehabilitation processes,*' *says Ian Saunders, co-founder of CryoAction, a UK company that supplies many top rugby and football teams with cryotherapy facilities. 'Vasoconstriction reduces blood flow to the extremities, which reduces inflammation around soft-tissue injuries, stopping them progressing. The release of adrenalin relieves pain and generates the feelings of exhilaration that players report.*'
>
> **As quoted in**
> ***The Guardian*,**
> **24 July 2017**

→ *Whole-body cryotherapy is said to have played a decisive role in Leicester City winning the Premier League in 2016. Every player spent time each day in the club's cryotherapy chamber.*

## Electronic pulse massage systems

Electronic pulse massage systems pass a small electric current through pads attached to the skin, creating small involuntary muscle contractions. The pulsing current stimulates the muscle, improving blood flow through the muscle and reducing tension.

Electronic pulse massage systems can be used to treat muscle spasms and muscle pain. They can also be used to increase muscular strength after suffering a serious injury that has resulted in a significant loss of muscle mass.

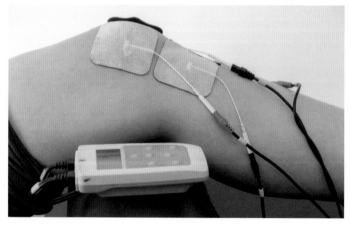

→ *Electronic pulse massage systems are inexpensive and can be used by people at home to relax their muscles, relieve pain and increase muscular strength.*

## Hyperbaric oxygen treatment

Only 21 per cent of the air we breathe normally is oxygen. Hyperbaric oxygen treatment involves breathing 100 per cent oxygen in a pressurized chamber, bringing much more oxygen into the body than normal with every breath. The oxygen enters into all the body's fluids, not just the red blood cells, and is carried to areas where blood flow is limited because of injury or disease. This extra oxygen helps white blood cells fight infection, reduces swelling, and promotes healing.

Hyperbaric oxygen treatment has traditionally been used to treat divers who have surfaced too quickly and are suffering from decompression illness. It is now being used to treat a wider range of conditions, including serious infections and wounds that will not heal. Some also advocate its use to treat sports injuries.

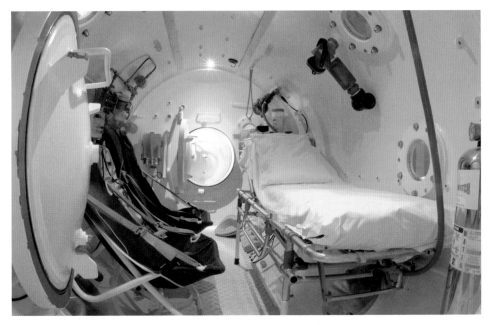

➜ *A patient breathes 100 per cent oxygen in a hyperbaric oxygen chamber.*

## Resistance bands

Made from elastic, resistance bands are a low-cost technology that can be used to increase muscular strength after an injury. They come in different resistances, allowing you to gently increase the force you are working with as your rehabilitation progresses. They cause minimal stress to joints and are particularly useful in the early stages of rehabilitation when people struggle to put weight through a joint.

➜ *Resistance bands come in two different types: some with handles, some without.*

**G old**

3. Imagine that you have fractured your tibia playing hockey.

   **a)** Analyse which of the technological rehabilitation techniques discussed here – whole-body cryotherapy, electronic pulse massage systems, hyperbaric oxygen treatment and resistance bands – will most help your recovery.

   **b)** Blend the technological rehabilitation technique you have chosen with basic rehabilitation techniques to create a rehabilitation plan.

# 1B Practice for Component 1, Learning aim B assignment

**Learning aim B:** Explore common injuries in sport and activity and methods of rehabilitation

## Scenario

You have just started work at a local leisure centre, helping coaching staff to run sports and activity sessions. You have been asked to prepare a series of leaflets advising the team on the symptoms, causes, and treatment of common sporting injuries.

## Task

Prepare two leaflets, one on a basic sporting injury of your choice and one on a complex sporting injury of your choice. The leaflets should discuss the symptoms of the injuries, how the injuries might be caused, what a sports leader can do to minimize the risk to participants, and how a first aider should respond, and include a rehabilitation plan to ensure the injured participant makes a full recovery. Your leaflets should:

→ Identify some common sporting injuries, their symptoms, and possible causes (B.1P3).

→ Outline common sporting injuries, their symptoms, and possible causes (B.1M3).

→ Describe common sporting injuries, their causes, and related rehabilitation (B.2P3).

→ Explain, using clear sporting examples, how sports injuries may occur and suggest rehabilitation (B.2M2).

→ Analyse common sports injuries in a chosen sport or activity, recommending rehabilitation, including the use of technology (B.2D2).

## Tackling the assignment

Remember to produce two leaflets, one about a basic sporting injury and one about a complex sporting injury. If you are aiming for a Level 2 Distinction, then you should think about your chosen injuries in the context of one specific sport.

Begin each leaflet by describing (if you are aiming for a Level 2 Pass), explaining (if you are aiming for a Level 2 Merit), or analysing (if you are aiming for a Level 2 Distinction) your chosen injury and its symptoms.

Next, each leaflet should describe, explain, or analyse how the injury can occur, what sports leaders should do to minimize the likelihood of participants suffering from the injury, and how a first aider should respond if a participant is hurt.

Finally, each leaflet should describe, explain, or analyse basic rehabilitation techniques and the use of technology in rehabilitation and come up with a rehabilitation plan to help a participant suffering from the injury to make a full recovery.

- When you <u>describe</u> something, you give a clear account of it in your own words. You should go into detail, and could include some photographs or drawings to illustrate your description.
- When you <u>explain</u> something, you need to provide examples or evidence to illustrate your description or provide reasons that tell the reader why it is like it is, so remember to include sporting examples throughout.
- When you <u>analyse</u> something, you need to structure your work carefully so that the reader is introduced to each point you want to make in a logical order. You need to provide lots of detail and you need to explore an issue from all angles.

## Meeting the Level 2 Pass criteria

# Tendonitis

Tendonitis is an injury that happens to tendons which become inflamed. Tendons join muscle to bone at a joint, so tendonitis occurs at joints.

Tendonitis causes pain when exercising and often causes pain first thing in the morning because the inflammation builds up overnight when the joint is still.

Tendonitis can be an overuse injury. The tendons can be overworked by doing too much too soon.

This learner has given a clear description of one complex sporting injury. The injury and its symptoms and causes are clearly described. The description would be even better if the learner included a photograph, perhaps an image of a tennis player with a caption saying that tennis elbow is tendonitis that occurs at the elbow.

If this learner continues in the same way, describing what sports leaders should do to minimize the likelihood of participants suffering from the injury, how a first aider should respond, and how the injury can be rehabilitated, they will meet the criteria for a Level 2 Pass.

## Meeting the **Level 2 Merit** criteria

### Strain

A strain is an injury that occurs to muscles or tendons when they are stretched beyond their normal range. Depending on the severity of the injury, a strain will cause pain, some swelling, tenderness, and loss of movement. It will be particularly painful when trying to contract the muscle that has been damaged or the muscle attached to the tendon that has been damaged.

Sports performers can strain their Achilles tendon. This causes great pain in the gastrocnemius when weight is put on the leg or when the toes are pointed. The Achilles tendon transmits force from the gastrocnemius muscles to the ankle, allowing us to jump or sprint, and these activities will be particularly difficult for people who have strained the Achilles tendon or their gastrocnemius muscles.

Sports where Achilles strains can happen involve sprinting or jumping from a standing start, such as the long jump or the triple jump, or any sport where people land on hard surfaces, such as netball when receiving a pass while jumping or volleyball when landing from a spike shot.

> This learner has given a clear description of one simple sporting injury and its symptoms. If the learner were to continue in this way, they would meet the Level 2 Pass criteria. They have, however, gone further.

> This learner has gone on to explain how the injury is caused, providing detailed sporting examples. If the learner continues in this way, explaining what sports leaders should do to minimize the likelihood of participants suffering from the injury and how a first aider should respond if a participant is hurt, as well as explaining how the injury should be rehabilitated, they will meet the criteria for a Level 2 Merit.

## Meeting the **Level 2 Distinction** criteria

### A leaflet on dislocation for rugby players

**What is a dislocation and when is it most likely to occur?**

A dislocated shoulder is a particularly traumatic injury because the humerus pops out of the socket of the shoulder joint. The injury causes a great deal of pain immediately and there will be a loss of function making it difficult to move or raise the arm. It may also be possible to see an obvious deformity, and the arm will feel numb and may tingle. There may be swelling present because the dislocation can damage muscles and ligaments in the shoulder, creating bleeding and inflammation. In rugby, the injury often occurs when a player falls on their arm when it is raised or when they are tackled.

There are a number of risk factors that increase the risk of the injury for rugby players. Freezing temperatures make the ground very hard, which means the impact is more severe when players fall or are tackled. The cold weather also means that players may not have warmed up fully. Extending warm-ups in cold weather can help to minimize the risk of dislocation by ensuring that players are physically and mentally prepared for what follows.

**What to do if a player experiences a dislocation**

> It is important to structure an analysis logically, and headings help to create a logical structure.

> This learner is analysing the causes of the injury, and exploring, in detail, a range of situations when a rugby player might experience a dislocation, and how a sports leader can minimize the risk of this happening.

> The learner plans to analyse how a dislocated shoulder should be managed. If the learner then goes on to analyse how the injury should be rehabilitated, they will meet the criteria for a Level 2 Distinction.

Technology has a huge impact on sport and physical activity. To take just one example, in 1970, the average distance a professional golfer could hit a golf ball with a drive was 225 yards; today the average distance is 295 yards. Some of this increase is almost certainly down to better training and improved technique, but most is down to technological innovations to golf balls and to the size of club heads. Yet for all the benefits that performers, coaches and managers, and officials experience from advances in technology, there are limitations to the improvements in performance that technology can deliver. Using technology does also have some potential disadvantages.

## Equipment: technological advances, and their benefits and limitations

Tennis rackets have changed over the decades. Originally, tennis rackets were made of wood but, during the 1970s, manufacturers introduced tennis rackets made of steel. Today, most tennis rackets are made of graphite.

> Graphite tennis rackets, generally weighing around 300 grams, are lighter than steel tennis rackets and considerably lighter than wooden tennis rackets. Graphite is also incredibly strong, which means manufacturers are able to create lightweight tennis rackets with large heads, producing a larger sweet spot and allowing players to hit the ball with greater power.

> Wooden tennis rackets were heavy and flexible, weighing 370–400 grams. The sweet spot – the spot on the racket where the ball is propelled with most power and least vibration – tended to be small.

> Steel tennis rackets were lighter and stiffer than wooden tennis rackets, weighing about 350 grams. This allowed players to swing the racket more quickly and hit the ball with greater power and accuracy.

The game of tennis has changed as a result of the technological changes to tennis rackets. Players can swing lighter graphite rackets much more quickly than heavier wooden rackets. This speed, coupled with the greater stiffness of graphite rackets, means that the ball is flying through the air much faster than it used to. This is why the modern game is referred to as a power game. Some argue that the game is less skilful and graceful than it used to be and watching players 'slug it out' from the baseline makes a modern tennis match less of a spectacle, but the game is faster and more consistent today than it used to be.

### Other examples of technological advances in equipment
- Footballs used to be made of leather and held together with cotton lacing. Today they are made of polyurethane or polyvinyl chloride, stitched around a rubber or rubber-like air bladder.
- Goalposts used to be made of wood. Then many were made of steel. Aluminium is now the material of choice. The shape of the posts has also changed over time, from square to round to elliptical.
- Weight-training equipment used to consist of cast-iron barbells and dumb-bells. Today, many gyms have fixed-path resistance machines alongside free weights.

### B ronze

1. Choose one technological example from the 'Other examples of technological advances in equipment' box and find out more about it.

   a) Why did the technological advance come about? What problem with the equipment did technology set out to fix?

   b) What benefits did the new technology bring?

   c) Does the new technology have any disadvantages?

# Protection: technological advances, and their benefits and limitations

Phillip Hughes, an Australian cricketer, died of a brain haemorrhage in 2014 after he was hit on the neck by a cricket ball while batting during a match in Sydney.

Phillip was wearing a Masuri helmet when the fatal ball hit him. Since his death, Masuri have redesigned their helmet to offer batsmen more protection.

After Phillip's death, Cricket Australia commissioned a review that concluded that all batsmen should wear protective helmets when facing fast and medium-paced bowling. However, the review also found that Phillip would not have survived even if he had been wearing a helmet that meets the latest safety standards. Protective equipment can reduce your risk of injury but it cannot eliminate the risk of injury altogether; protective equipment does have its limitations.

→ *The adapted Masuri helmet has a 'StemGuard', which is padding that is clipped onto the visor to protect the neck. Masuri claim that the StemGuard is strong enough to protect batsmen from serious injury but light enough that it will not distract players from the game or make it more difficult for them to move freely.*

## Other examples of technological advances in protection

- In 1890, a London dentist invented a mouth guard to protect boxers from getting their lips cut. It was made from gutta-percha, a latex that comes from a Malaysian tree, and the boxer had to hold it in place by biting on it. Today, mouth guards are used by performers in a wide range of sports, including boxing, rugby, and hockey.
- Many scientific experiments, some involving crash-test dummies, have contributed to the manufacture of landing mats that can absorb the energy of the human body when it falls in specific sporting situations and keep performers safe from injury.

### S ilver

2.  Look at this photograph. Some of the hockey players are wearing protective face masks, some are not.

    Using the photograph for inspiration, debate these two statements:

    a) Players should always wear protective equipment even if it is not compulsory.

    b) Protective equipment makes players more reckless with their own safety and with the safety of others.

# Clothing: technological advances, and their benefits and limitations

Aerodynamics is the study of the way air moves over a moving object and the forces that the moving air and the moving object exert on each other. Drag is the name given to the resistance that the moving object experiences when it moves through the air. Given that many sporting events involve moving an object – a person, a person and a machine, a ball, and so on – through the air, the study of aerodynamics has had a huge impact on sport, and particularly on sporting clothing.

When Mark Cavendish won the UCI World Championships in 2011 he was wearing a skinsuit. The skintight suit is made of a smooth material that allows the air to pass around a cyclist's body without slowing down as much as it does otherwise, reducing drag and making the cyclist more aerodynamic. Mark and the seven other members of Team GB were the only cyclists wearing skinsuits that day, and Team GB is still leading the way in technological advances in aerodynamic clothing.

Ahead of the 2016 Rio Olympics, British Cycling revealed that its riders would be wearing a revolutionary new skinsuit, with chevron-shaped ridges on the backs of the arms and legs. It claimed the new suit had shaved three seconds off the team's 4km team pursuit time in training. This announcement will have given the team confidence and, consequently, a perceived psychological edge over their competitors.

→ *Technology undoubtedly contributed to Team GB's medal haul at the 2016 Rio Olympic Games, where they won six gold medals.*

## Other examples of technological advances in clothing

- Many runners now wear compression socks and many rugby players wear compression clothing. It is believed the technology helps to prevent injuries and speeds up recovery after training, although there is little scientific evidence to prove this.
- Some clothing fibres wick moisture better than others. This means they absorb the moisture created by the body when the wearer – a performer, coach, manager, or official – sweats. Manufacturers claim moisture control clothing helps wearers regulate their temperature but, again, there is little scientific evidence to back up the claims.

## B ronze/Silver

3. Swimming's world governing body, FINA, banned swimmers from wearing full-length, hi-tech swimsuits from 1 January 2010. Find out why and decide whether or not you think FINA made the right decision.

# Footwear: technological advances, and their benefits and limitations

The first football boots were made from strong leather and were designed to protect the wearer from injury. Players continued to wear heavy, protective boots until the 1950s, when manufacturers started to develop lighter, more flexible footwear that allowed players to control the ball with more finesse. Technological advances mean that boots have been getting lighter and more flexible ever since, so much so that many argue that many boots on the market today offer the wearer very little protection.

→ *These football boots are made of hard, heavy leather and are designed to protect the ankle. Rounded studs were hammered into the bottom of the boots.*

→ *The soles of football boots began to be made with synthetic materials, rather than leather, from the 1950s. This made the sole more flexible and enabled manufacturers to develop screw-in studs.*

→ *By the 1990s football boots were cut lower and available in a range of colours. Players were signing sponsorship deals with football boot manufacturers. Adidas pioneered the use of rubber blades rather than moulded or screw-in studs, allowing greater grip.*

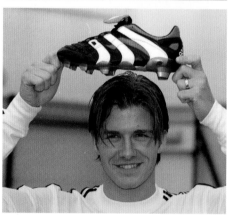

→ *Technology will continue to play an important role in the development of the football boot. This 'smart boot' contains sensors that monitor how the ball is kicked, providing the player with feedback they can use to develop their technique.*

## Other examples of technological advances in footwear

- Insoles can be slotted into a shoe to provide the wearer with more comfort and support. They can also help to ensure that a wearer's foot lands correctly on the ground, protecting them from injury and improving their performance.
- Leather footwear absorbs water and can become very heavy. The first shoes and boots made out of waterproof material were lighter, but the wearer's feet could get very sticky and sweaty. Modern waterproof materials, such as GORE-TEX®, are breathable, making shoes and boots much more comfortable to wear.

**S ilver**

4. The introduction of studs was a technological innovation. Design and carry out an experiment to analyse the impact studs have on speed and agility.

## Facilities: technological advances, and their benefits and limitations

Artificial grass has come a long way since the first AstroTurf pitches were laid in the 1960s. Second generation, or 2G, pitches have sand infill and are perfect for games such as hockey. Third generation, or 3G, pitches have rubber crumb infill and are better for football, Gaelic football, and rugby. Some manufacturers are also offering fourth generation, or 4G, pitches, which do not have any infill at all, but as yet none of these have been approved for use by any sport's governing body.

Artificial grass does not need to be mown regularly like real grass, but it does need to be maintained. The infill needs to be topped up, repairs need to be made to the surface, and the surface needs to be brushed and cleaned. This maintenance can be expensive. Artificial grass also wears out and needs to be replaced, unlike real grass that keeps growing.

Artificial pitches do not get muddy in the rain, and are consistently flat. 3G pitches also provide players with better grip and absorb shock better than real grass pitches. However, concerns have been raised about the type and number of injuries picked up on artificial pitches. Players can suffer more serious skin burns playing on artificial pitches than they will if they play on grass pitches. Furthermore, the Rugby Football Union analysed the number of injuries recorded during the 2017–2018 Premiership season and the official report stated that, 'The burden of injuries on artificial turf pitches is higher than those on natural grass (natural grass, 2433 days absence per 1000 hours; artificial turf 3015 days absence per 1000 hours).' That's a big difference.

### Other examples of technological advances in facilities

- Technology enables participants to control the air temperature of their indoor playing spaces with air conditioning and heating. It can also improve ventilation, drawing in fresh air from outside into a building. Controlling the climate can make participants feel more comfortable and can help them perform to the best of their ability.
- Sprung floors absorb shock, helping to improve performance and prevent injuries. Anti-friction floors help to prevent people from slipping, falling, and hurting themselves. Both have benefited from technological advancements. Technology has even engineered safer, more durable wooden floors.

### Bronze

5. Carry out an audit of the flooring in the indoor playing spaces at your school or a local sports centre.

   a) Identify what each floor is made from.

   b) Explain the benefits of each floor. How does it facilitate the activities that take place on it?

   c) Choose one floor you identified during your audit. Can new technology make the floor better for the activities that it is used for? Carry out some research and explain your findings.

# Cameras, computers, and software, and their benefits and limitations

The impact of technology on sport and physical activity is most obvious when it comes to cameras, computers, and software. Here are just a few of the more recent developments:

→ *Cricket pioneered the use of Hawk-Eye™ and it is now regularly used in many other sports, including tennis and rugby. It is a computer system that uses multiple cameras to track the trajectory of the ball. The information is presented to officials to help them make decisions, and to viewers to enhance the viewing experience.*

→ *Goal line technology helps officials determine whether or not a football has crossed the goal line. Some systems use cameras and others use magnetic fields, but whichever approach is used, the referee receives a signal on their watch within one second of the goal so that play is not delayed.*

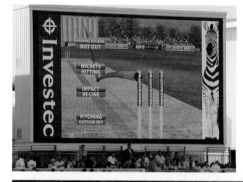

→ *Videoing a performance allows a participant or team and their coach or manager to analyse their performance. You can rewind a section of the performance and play it several times or you can pause the video to look closely at what is happening. Many software packages allow you to look at two screenshots or photographs side by side, to compare a participant's performance to a desired model or to see how a participant has progressed over time. The same technology can also be used to analyse the opposition's performance to work out their weak points in advance of a competition.*

→ *Wearable technology allows an individual participant, and their coach or manager, to collect data about their performance. For example, a heart rate monitor will collect data about how hard the participant is working at different points in the match or training session, and a GPS tracker will monitor the distance they cover and their average speed. Smartwatches and bra-like vest tops are examples of wearable technology. Apps allow people using wearable technology to access and analyse the data collected.*

6. Take a photograph of a partner in the 'set' position of a sprint start. Take the photograph from the side, so that you can compare the image with the photograph here.

   What differences can you see between this photograph and the one you have taken? Consider:

   • the height of the hips in relation to the shoulders
   • the angle at the hips
   • the angles at the knees.

Cameras, computers, and software have huge benefits for performers, coaches and managers, and officials. They also have some limitations and disadvantages.

|  | **Benefits** | **Limitations and disadvantages** |
|---|---|---|
| **Performers** | • Performers can monitor their cardiorespiratory system and adjust their training programme to ensure they are working in the appropriate training zone to deliver progressive overload but are not overtraining.<br>• Performers can use video-analysis software and other data collected to analyse the way they perform skills and adjust their technique to improve their performance.<br>• Skills analysis can allow performers to focus their training on specific parts of their musculoskeletal system, in order to make marginal gains that will give them an advantage over competitors.<br>• Data collected during rehabilitation can help a performer return to full health and get back to participating in sport and physical activity quickly after an injury. | • Data collected from wearable technology can influence the decisions coaches and managers make, and not always to the advantage of a performer or a team. For example, players that are good at reading a game may not move as much as players who are less good at reading a game, but their coach may analyse the data collected and decide they are not working hard enough to earn their place on the team.<br>• Data collected can be used to compare players on a team, and this is not always appropriate. For example, the data will not show the different role each player has in a team or the tactical demands of their opponents.<br>• Injured performers can become over-reliant on data collected using technology, delaying their return to sport and physical activity until the data say they are well, and forgetting that how they feel is the very best indicator of when they are ready to start exercising again. |

| Coaches and managers | • Coaches can monitor individual performers' cardiorespiratory systems and design training programmes to deliver progressive overload without encouraging overtraining. This is particularly useful for coaches who work with teams, because different players will have different requirements. For example, a lower than average heart rate during the main component of a training session may suggest the performer is not receiving adequate overload, while a higher than normal resting heart rate may suggest a performer is overdoing it.<br>• Data about how performers' cardiorespiratory systems are working can help coaches choose the fittest players for a squad or for a match during a competition. It can also help them work out if a team is performing as well as it should during a match.<br>• Coaches can use video-analysis software to analyse the way individuals perform skills so they can provide guidance on how the individual can adjust their technique to improve their performance.<br>• Coaches can use video-analysis software to analyse how a team works together, which can help them design training sessions that work on eliminating weaknesses. | • It can be time consuming to collect and analyse data, drawing a coach's attention away from actual coaching.<br>• Technology cannot replace a coach's instinct. For example, Lionel Messi may never have played professional football if the coaches who worked with him when he was young had relied purely on the data they collected; he would have been considered too small and too slow.<br>• Technology moves very fast and it can be difficult for coaches to stay up-to-date with the latest developments and share them with performers.<br>• The latest technology is expensive, which means that some performers and some teams may not be able to afford it. This can put a coach at a disadvantage, especially if their competitors do have access to the benefits technology has to offer.<br>• Technology can sometimes go wrong, which can be frustrating. Repair costs can also be expensive. |
|---|---|---|
| Officials | • Technology can help officials make more accurate decisions.<br>• Officials can collect data about their cardiovascular performance, just like performers, and can use the data to determine whether or not they are fit enough to keep up with the action. | • Breaks in play, while officials wait to receive information from technology such as VAR, can disrupt the flow of the game. This is particularly evident in football, where it can be frustrating for spectators and players. If players have to stand and wait for a decision for a particularly long time, their heart rates and breathing rates will decrease and they may lose the momentum and concentration they have developed.<br>• Most state-of-the-art technology, such as goal line technology, is only available at elite levels even though it would be useful to grass-roots officials. |

**Ⓛ Link**

Progressive overload and training zones are discussed on pages 73–78. Overtraining is discussed on page 79.

# 1C  Practice for Component 1, Learning aim C assignment

## Scenario

In your role as an assistant coach for a local sports team, you have been asked to prepare a report into the latest technological developments affecting everyone involved with the team. The head coach would like to know which technological developments will help the team perform better, as well as increase participation in training and competition.

## Task

Prepare a report exploring the advantages and disadvantages of four technological developments in sport. Your report should consider the impact of the developments on performers, coaches and managers, and officials, and include specific sporting examples. Your report should:

→ Identify some types of technology used in sport and activity, showing some understanding of their usage (C.1P4).

→ Outline different types of technology used in sport and activity, showing an understanding of their usage using sporting examples (C.1M4).

→ Describe, using sporting examples, different types of technology used in sport and activity, clearly describing their usage, along with identification of benefits and limitations (C.2P4).

→ Analyse, using sporting examples, the different types of technology used in sport and activity, along with an explanation of benefits and limitations (C.2M3).

→ Assess the benefits and limitations of technological advances in sport and activity, using clear sporting examples (C.2D3).

## Tackling the assignment

Begin your report by introducing the four technological advancements you are going to investigate. Then work through each one in turn.

If you are aiming for a Level 2 Pass, you need to describe each technological advancement and identify its advantages/benefits and its disadvantages/limitations. When you <u>describe</u> something, you give a clear account of it in your own words. You should go into detail, and could include some photographs or drawings to illustrate your description. When you <u>identify</u> something, you list the key points. Remember to consider performers, coaches and managers, and officials.

If you are aiming for a Level 2 Merit, you need to analyse each technological advancement and explain its advantages/benefits and its disadvantages/limitations.

When you <u>analyse</u> something, you need to structure your work carefully so that the reader is introduced to each point you want to make in a logical order. You need to provide lots of detail, including relevant examples, and you need to explore an issue from all angles. When you <u>explain</u> something, you need to provide examples or evidence to illustrate your list of key points. Again, remember to consider performers, coaches and managers, and officials.

If you are aiming for a Level 2 Distinction, you need to <u>assess</u> the advantages/benefits and disadvantages/limitations of each technological advancement. This means that you need to describe each technological advancement, then go on to look at its pros and cons and come to a conclusion as to whether or not it benefits performers, coaches and managers, and officials.

## Meeting the **Level 2 Pass** criteria

However, Hawk-Eye™ does have its limitations. Officials have to wait to receive information from the technology and this causes breaks in play, which can be frustrating for players. Also, the technology is only available at elite level, and sometimes only in specific categories of competition, which means that some officials have to do their job without the support it provides.

> This learner has identified two problems with Hawk-Eye™. If the learner has already described what Hawk-Eye™ is and what it does, and has identified its benefits to performers, coaches and managers, and officials, then they will meet the criteria for a Level 2 Pass if they also cover three other technological developments to a similar depth.

## Meeting the **Level 2 Merit** criteria

However, Hawk-Eye™ does have a number of limitations for officials. When receiving information on-field officials must wait, often for an off-field official to inform them of a decision. This creates breaks in play and interrupts the flow of a game, which can be frustrating for players and affects spectators' enjoyment. For example, in rugby, it is common for a team to score and the team and spectators to celebrate wildly, only for everyone to have to wait for confirmation from an off-field video referee that a try was scored. This can create additional tension, but it does seem to take something away from the elation shared by the scorer and the crowd. It also slows down the opposition's restart if the referee

> This learner has explained one problem with Hawk-Eye™. Compare the level of detail provided by this learner with the level of detail provided by the learner who identified two problems to meet the Level 2 Pass criteria. This learner has provided a detailed example to support the problem they have identified.

was inclined not to award a try but checked with the video referee rather than trusting his instinct. The delay gives the 'scoring' team time to regroup, rather than allowing the opposition to mount a swift counter-attack.

If the learner has already analysed what Hawk-Eye™ is and what it does, and has explained its benefits to performers, coaches and managers, and officials, then they will meet the criteria for a Level 2 Merit if they also explain at least one more problem with Hawk-Eye™ and cover three other technological developments to a similar depth.

## Meeting the **Level 2 Distinction** criteria

However, Hawk-Eye™ does have a number of limitations. The breaks in play that are seen in tennis, when an official or a player calls for a review of the video evidence, mean matches lose momentum. This is not to suggest that the technology should not be used. It would be valuable if, for example, service calls in tennis were automated to help officials make quicker line calls, perhaps on the baseline. But the technology also seems to be affecting the way the game is played. Players in long rallies who are under pressure have been known to call for a review even if they know the line judge's decision was good, just to buy time or frustrate their opponent. Players are allowed three challenges per set and when a set is drawing to a close they tend to speculatively use up their challenges. Although this is perfectly legal, it does seem to not be in the spirit of the game and perhaps the tennis authorities need to consider implementing rules against tactical use of video replays.

This learner has explored two problems with Hawk-Eye™ in depth. Notice that the discussion in the first paragraph in particular is much more sophisticated than the work produced by the learner explaining a problem to meet the Level 2 Merit criteria.

Some have argued that referring decisions to video referees undermines the authority of the on-field officials and that players trust their decisions less and are less respectful than they used to be as a result. This mistrust may also filter down to lower levels of the game, where the technology is not available to help officials, causing players to question decisions that have not gone their way more openly than they might have done in the past.

Overall, technology to assist officials, such as Hawk-Eye™, is beneficial because spectators have a greater appreciation of how difficult it is to make decisions. When watching football, it is interesting to see players protesting wildly against a linesman's decision only to see the official proved correct on video replay. Perhaps, as the technology gets cheaper, it will become available at lower levels. In the meantime, its use to support officials at elite level helps ensure that crucial decisions are got right.

This learner has ended their discussion of the problems with Hawk-Eye™ by coming to a conclusion about whether, on balance, they think its use is positive or negative. It is essential to do this if you want to meet the Level 2 Distinction criteria.

If the learner has already assessed what Hawk-Eye™ is and what it does, and has explored its benefits to performers, coaches and managers, and officials, then they will meet the criteria for a Level 2 Distinction if they cover three other technological developments to a similar depth.

# 2 The principles of training, nutrition, and psychology for sport and activity

Jake enjoys physical activity of all kinds. He plays football with his friends whenever he can and he practises judo. He is currently a 2nd Kyu and has his eyes set on a coveted black belt. He has recently begun to realize how important a healthy mind and body are to success in sport. He has heard his coaches talking about the principles of training and wants to find out how they can help him get fitter and better at judo. He also wants to eat more healthily and to learn how to harness the power of psychology to help him increase his motivation and self-confidence, and manage the anxiety he sometimes feels when he is competing.

This chapter will explore:

**Learning aim A: Training to improve fitness for sport and activity**

➜ 2.A1 Interpreting fitness data in relation to sport and activity

➜ 2.A2 Methods of training for sport and activity

➜ 2.A3 The FITT principles and principles of training

➜ 2.A4 Understanding fitness programmes

**Learning aim B: Nutrition for sport and activity**

➜ 2.B1 Macronutrients

➜ 2.B2 Micronutrients

➜ 2.B3 Hydration

➜ 2.B4 Improving nutrition for sport and activity

**Learning aim C: The psychological influence that motivation, self-confidence, and anxiety have on participation in sport and activity**

➜ 2.C1 The impact of motivation on participation in sport and activity

➜ 2.C2 The impact self-confidence can have on participation in sport and activity

➜ 2.C3 The impact of anxiety on participation in sport and activity

Physical fitness is your general ability to meet the physical demands placed on you by the environment, and it can be broken down into seven components of fitness. It is possible to measure your level of fitness in each component of fitness, and to use this information to determine how successful you are likely to be at a range of sports and physical activities.

## The components of fitness

The seven components of fitness are:

Muscular endurance

Flexibility

Aerobic endurance

Strength

Speed

Power

Body composition

Each component of fitness describes a specific aspect of sporting performance. Success in different sports requires different combinations of these components. Some sports need performers to develop a high level of fitness in just one or two components, while other sports, including games activities, require performers to develop a high level of fitness in many different components in order to excel.

Fitness tests are used to measure a performer's level of fitness in each component of fitness.

# Aerobic endurance

**Aerobic endurance** is the ability of the cardiovascular system to deliver oxygenated blood to the working muscles and to remove waste products, such as carbon dioxide and lactic acid. It is, in other words, a measure of the body's ability to release energy aerobically.

Aerobic endurance is particularly important for activities that take place over an extended period of time, including marathon running, endurance cycling, long-distance swimming, and long-distance rowing.

## Testing aerobic endurance: the Cooper 12-minute run test

**Objective:** Run as far as you can in 12 minutes.

**Protocol:**

- Conduct a suitable warm-up, if necessary.
- Use a stopwatch to accurately time the test.
- Using a 400-metre running track, count the number of laps and part laps you complete in 12 minutes.
- Calculate how many metres you travelled in 12 minutes, rounding down to the nearest metre.

> Normative data show the results for the general population. Data are collected from a lot of people and the most common results are established. You can compare your results to normative data to establish your level of fitness in the component of fitness being tested.

**Normative data:**

| Gender | Excellent | Above average | Average | Below average | Poor |
|--------|-----------|---------------|---------|---------------|------|
| Male | > 2800m | 2500–2800m | 2300–2499m | 2200–2299m | < 2200m |
| Female | > 2100m | 2000–2100m | 1700–1999m | 1600–1699m | < 1600m |

> > means 'more than' and < means 'less than'. These symbols are often used in normative data tables.

# Muscular endurance

**Muscular endurance** is a measure of how long a performer's muscles can powerfully contract repeatedly before they suffer fatigue. It relies on the body's ability to deliver oxygen and remove lactic acid.

Muscular endurance is especially important for endurance athletes, such as rowers, cyclists, and runners, and is also needed by games players.

## Testing muscular endurance: the one-minute sit-up test

**Objective:** Perform as many sit-ups as possible in one minute to demonstrate the muscular endurance of core muscles.

### Protocol:

- Conduct a suitable warm-up, if necessary.
- Use a stopwatch to accurately time the test.
- Ensure you know the correct technique for a sit-up. Only correctly performed sit-ups count.
- Establish the correct start position, on an appropriate surface.
- Count how many sit-ups you can complete in one minute. You may only rest in the starting position.

### Normative data:

| Gender | Excellent | Above average | Average | Below average | Poor |
|--------|-----------|---------------|---------|---------------|------|
| Male | > 49 | 43–48 | 36–42 | 31–35 | < 30 |
| Female | > 42 | 36–41 | 29–35 | 24–28 | < 23 |

The correct technique for a sit-up is as follows:

1. Lie on your back, with your knees bent and your feet about hip distance apart.
2. Choose a position for your hands: cross your arms and place your hands on opposite shoulders, or place your hands just behind your ears without pulling on your neck.
3. Curl your body all the way up towards your knees, exhaling as you do so.
4. Lower yourself to the starting point, inhaling as you do so.

# Flexibility

**Flexibility** is the ability to move your joints through their full range of motion smoothly. The more flexible you are, the easier it is for you to move your body into sporting positions and the less likely you are to injure yourself.

Flexibility is important in many sports and physical activities. For example, good flexibility allows dancers and gymnasts to move their bodies into unusual positions. It also allows games players to execute dynamic movements, such as kicking a football or hitting a golf ball.

## Testing flexibility: the sit-and-reach test
**Objective:** Reach as far as possible to demonstrate flexibility at the hip.

### Protocol:
- Conduct a suitable warm-up, if necessary.
- Sit on the floor with your legs straight in front of you. You should have bare feet.
- Put the soles of your feet, shoulder width apart, against the sit-and-reach box. Make sure your knees are flat against the floor.
- Reach gently forwards, towards and beyond your feet, with your hands on top of each other and your palms facing down. Reach as far as possible, taking care not to bounce.
- After three practice reaches, hold the fourth reach for at least two seconds.
- The distance in centimetres (cm) that your fingers touch on the sit-and-reach box is your score.

### Normative data:

| Gender | Excellent | Above average | Average | Below average | Poor |
|---|---|---|---|---|---|
| Male | > 41cm | 33–41cm | 25–32cm | 13–24cm | < 13cm |
| Female | > 46cm | 38–46cm | 29–37cm | 19–28cm | < 19cm |

# Speed

**Speed** is the rate at which an individual is able to perform a movement or cover a distance.

Speed is generally associated with sprinting, because the more speed someone has, the quicker they can cover the ground. However, performing a sporting action at high speed is important for many activities, including throwing a fast punch in boxing, sprinting towards the try line in rugby, or performing a fast break in basketball.

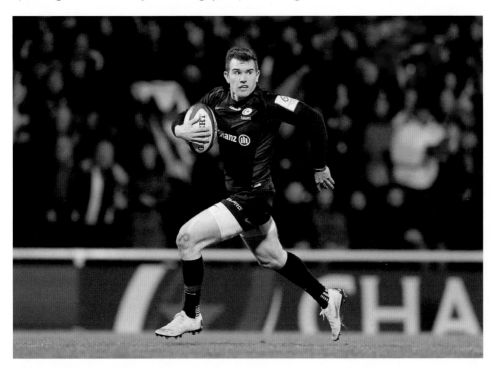

## Testing speed: the 30-metre sprint test

**Objective:** Sprint 30 metres as quickly as possible, given a flying start.

**Protocol:**

- Conduct a suitable warm-up, if necessary.
- Select a suitable sprinting area, about 70–80 metres long.
- Mark a distance of 30 metres, using two marker cones, near the middle of the sprinting area.
- Accelerate towards the first cone, so that you are running at your maximum speed as you pass it. Continue running, as fast as you can, past the second cone.
- Use a stopwatch to accurately time the test. A stopwatch is started as you pass the first cone and stopped as you pass the second cone. The time is recorded in seconds, to one decimal place.

**Normative data:**

| Gender | Excellent | Above average | Average | Below average | Poor |
|--------|-----------|---------------|---------|---------------|------|
| Male | < 4.0 seconds | 4.0–4.2 seconds | 4.3–4.4 seconds | 4.5–4.6 seconds | > 4.6 seconds |
| Female | < 4.5 seconds | 4.5–4.6 seconds | 4.7–4.8 seconds | 4.9–5.0 seconds | > 5.0 seconds |

## Strength

**Strength** is the amount of force muscles can generate to overcome resistance.

In sport, strength can be used to lift a weight, as in weightlifting or rock climbing, or to hold your body in a given position, as in gymnastics.

### Testing strength: the hand grip dynamometer test

**Objective:** Generate the highest possible force reading on the grip dynamometer to demonstrate grip strength.

**Protocol:**

- Use a grip dynamometer.
- Record the highest reading from three attempts, using your dominant hand and allowing a one-minute rest between attempts.
- Grip strength is usually measured in kilograms (kg).

**Normative data:**

| Gender | Excellent | Above average | Average | Below average | Poor |
|--------|-----------|---------------|---------|---------------|------|
| Male | > 52kg | 47–51kg | 44–46kg | 39–43kg | < 39kg |
| Female | > 32kg | 28–31kg | 25–27kg | 20–24kg | < 20kg |

# Power

**Power** is the ability to combine strength and speed.

The ability to contract muscles quickly, with great strength, is used in sport to power out of the block and through the drive phase in a sprint race, to hit a ball with great power in golf and racket sports, and to jump powerfully in athletics, basketball, and netball. For example, a high jumper generates power from their lower body to drive off the ground and over the bar.

## Testing power: the sergeant jump test

**Objective:** Jump as high as possible to demonstrate power in your lower body.

**Protocol:**

- Conduct a suitable warm-up, if necessary.
- Stand side-on to a wall and reach up with the hand closest to the wall. Keeping your feet flat on the ground, mark or measure the highest point on the wall your fingertips can touch. This is your standing reach.
- Put chalk on your fingertips. Stand away from the wall and jump vertically as high as possible, using both arms and legs to help you propel your body upwards. Touch the wall at the highest point of the jump.
- Measure the distance in centimetres (cm) between your standing reach and the highest point reached after three jumps.

**Normative data:**

| Gender | Excellent | Above average | Average | Below average | Poor |
|--------|-----------|---------------|---------|---------------|------|
| Male | > 60cm | 50–60cm | 40–49cm | 30–39cm | < 30cm |
| Female | > 55cm | 45–55cm | 35–44cm | 25–34cm | < 25cm |

# Body composition

**Body composition** is a measure of the percentages of fat, muscle, bone, water, and vital organs that make up your body weight. You are born with a tendency towards a particular body composition, but exercise and diet can bring about changes. The important thing is that you have the optimum body composition for your sport.

These performers both have the optimum body composition for their sport. The diver has low levels of body fat and smaller muscles, which means he can quickly manipulate his body into different positions before hitting the water. The sumo wrestler has high levels of body fat and large muscles, which means that he has a good chance of overcoming his opponent by pushing him out of the dohyo.

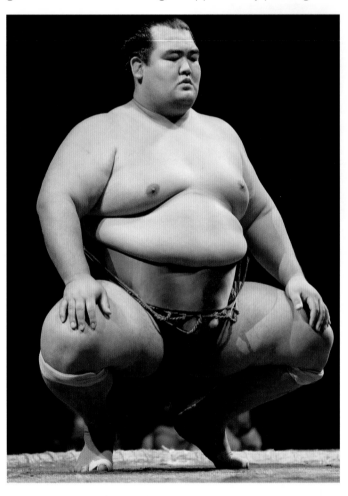

## B ronze/Silver

1. Use the information on pages 51–58 to help you with the following:

   a) Identify the components of fitness that are essential to success in one of your favourite sports or physical activities. Explain your decisions.

   b) Perform the appropriate fitness tests to assess the components of fitness that you identified in part a).

   c) Analyse the data you collect, comparing them against normative data. What conclusions can you draw? Which components of fitness are you strongest in and which are you weakest in? Which do you need to improve?

# Fitness testing and its impact for different target groups

When a performer knows which components of fitness are most important for their sport or physical activity, and what their level of fitness is in each of these components, they can design a training programme that suits their specific needs. Over time, if they follow the training programme, their fitness should improve and they should become better at their chosen sport or physical activity.

Fitness testing is not only useful for elite performers or fit and active people who are striving to improve their performance. It can also be used to help people manage rehabilitation from injury and to help younger people and older people determine the level they can participate at.

Generally, normative data measure what is normal for men and women across all age groups, but they can also be more targeted. For example, a 15-year-old boy can complete the sit-and-reach test and compare his test result with normative data for 15–16-year-old boys. Or a woman aged 65 can compare her hand grip dynamometer test result with the test results of other women over the age of 50. Comparing your data with more targeted normative data enables you to make a more accurate judgement about your level of fitness.

## B ronze/Silver

2. Look at the age-specific and gender-specific normative data for the Cooper 12-minute run test and then answer the questions below.

| Age | Gender | Excellent | Above average | Average | Below average | Poor |
|---|---|---|---|---|---|---|
| 13–14 | Male | > 2700m | 2400–2700m | 2200–2399m | 2100–2199m | < 2100m |
| | Female | > 2000m | 1900–2000m | 1600–1899m | 1500–1599m | < 1500m |
| 15–16 | Male | > 2800m | 2500–2800m | 2300–2499m | 2200–2299m | < 2200m |
| | Female | > 2100m | 2000–2100m | 1700–1999m | 1600–1699m | < 1600m |
| 17–19 | Male | > 3000m | 2700–3000m | 2500–2699m | 2300–2499m | < 2300m |
| | Female | > 2300m | 2100–2300m | 1800–2099m | 1700–1799m | < 1700m |
| 20–29 | Male | > 2800m | 2400–2800m | 2200–2399m | 1600–2199m | < 1600m |
| | Female | > 2700m | 2200–2700m | 1800–2199m | 1500–1799m | < 1500m |
| 30–39 | Male | > 2700m | 2300–2700m | 1900–2299m | 1500–1899m | < 1500m |
| | Female | > 2500m | 2000–2500m | 1700–1999m | 1400–1699m | < 1400m |
| 40–49 | Male | > 2500m | 2100–2500m | 1700–2099m | 1400–1699m | < 1400m |
| | Female | > 2300m | 1900–2300m | 1500–1899m | 1200–1499m | < 1200m |
| 50 + | Male | > 2400m | 2000–2400m | 1600–1999m | 1300–1599m | < 1300m |
| | Female | > 2200m | 1700–2200m | 1400–1699m | 1100–1399m | < 1100m |

Source: *www.coopertestchart.com*

a) Julie has taken part in the Cooper 12-minute run test. She is 30 years old and her result was 1700 metres. Which category does she fit into? Is her aerobic endurance excellent, above average, average, below average, or poor for her age and gender?

b) Derek has taken part in the Cooper 12-minute run test. He is 53 years old and his result was 1200 metres. Which category does he fit into?

c) Feng Mien is 20 years old and she has taken part in the Cooper 12-minute run test. Her result was 2755 metres. Which category does she fit into?

d) Based on Derek's result, what do you recommend Derek does? Explain your answer.

e) Based on Feng Mien's result, can you suggest a sport that she has the potential to perform successfully in? What other components of fitness would she need to perform successfully in this sport?

# 2.A2  Methods of training for sport and activity

There are a number of different methods of training a performer can include in their training programme. The method, or methods, they choose will depend on the component, or components, of fitness they have decided they need to improve as a result of fitness testing.

## Training methods to improve aerobic endurance

### Continuous training

Continuous training involves performing an activity at a steady intensity. Activities include running, swimming, cycling, walking, and rowing.

Beginners should start with 20 minutes of continuous training once a week and build up to training continuously for 30–45 minutes two to three times per week.

| Advantages of continuous training | Disadvantages of continuous training |
|---|---|
| • Does not require expensive equipment.<br>• Good for beginners because it is straightforward.<br>• Can mimic aspects of endurance performance.<br>• Good for development of aerobic endurance during preseason training or at the beginning of a training programme. | • Can become tedious because there is not much variety.<br>• Takes a long time.<br>• Does not improve anaerobic fitness. |

### Interval training

Interval training involves predetermined periods of work interspersed with predetermined periods of rest. The rest periods, which can consist of complete rest or lighter work, allow the performer to work at a very high intensity during the periods of work. As with continuous training, activities that lend themselves to interval training include running, swimming, cycling, walking, and rowing.

The nature of the recovery interval and the number of repetitions depend on the performer's fitness. The fitter the performer, the shorter and more active the recovery intervals, and the more work/rest cycles the performer should complete in a training session.

| Advantages of interval training | Disadvantages of interval training |
|---|---|
| • Does not require expensive equipment.<br>• Does not require long training sessions.<br>• Has been shown to increase aerobic endurance very quickly.<br>• Improves the body's ability to delay, and then cope with, the accumulation of lactic acid.<br>• Flexible, so can be adjusted to suit the needs of the performer. | • Performers need to be motivated to tolerate the discomfort of the high-intensity work periods.<br>• Longer recovery time between training sessions is needed than with less intense methods of training. |

# Fartlek training

Fartlek is a Swedish word meaning 'speed play' and Fartlek training is a form of road running or cross-country running that blends continuous and interval training. The exercise is ongoing, as with continuous training, but the intensity rises and falls, as with interval training. It is traditionally done outdoors, over a variety of terrains, with landmarks such as hills, trees, and street signs used to trigger a change of speed.

A Fartlek training session might consist of a jog for three or four minutes, followed by a 40-second sprint, followed by a 40-second walk, followed by five to six minutes of jogging, and so on. The performer 'plays' at increasing and decreasing their speed, in response to the world around them and how they are feeling.

| Advantages of Fartlek training | Disadvantages of Fartlek training |
|---|---|
| • Does not require expensive equipment.<br>• More interesting than continuous training and interval training.<br>• Has been shown to increase aerobic endurance very quickly.<br>• Improves the body's ability to delay, and then cope with, the accumulation of lactic acid.<br>• Flexible, so can be adjusted to suit the needs of the performer.<br>• A good form of training for sports and physical activities where the intensity changes, such as games activities. | • Performers need to be highly motivated to increase the intensity frequently enough and high enough.<br>• Performers need to be experienced to ensure a training session is adequately demanding but they do not overdo it. |

**B ronze**

1. Take part in a continuous training session, an interval training session, and a Fartlek training session. Can you add any more advantages and disadvantages to the lists?

# Training methods to improve muscular endurance

## Circuit training

Circuit training generally involves 6–10 different exercises, called stations, which are done one after another in a series. The exercises can be laid out in a circuit, so participants move from one station to the next without the need to move equipment. Participants perform a set number of repetitions of each exercise at its station, or perform each exercise at its station for a set period of time, before moving on to the next exercise. Depending on the participant's level of fitness, they may choose to execute the circuit more than once in a training session.

Typical circuit training exercises include press-ups, sit-ups, burpees, squat thrusts, mountain climbers, triceps dips, squats, shuttle runs, lunges, and skipping. When planning a circuit that works the whole body, it is often a good idea to alternate the body parts worked so that fatigue does not reduce the quality of the movements performed.

| Advantages of circuit training | Disadvantages of circuit training |
|---|---|
| • Can be used for a whole-body workout.<br>• Very flexible, so can be designed to meet the specific needs of participants.<br>• Groups of people can train together. | • Performers need to be motivated to tolerate the discomfort of the high-intensity work periods.<br>• Longer recovery time between training sessions is needed than with less intense types of training.<br>• Equipment is required for certain exercises. |

➜ *This circuit training session contains a number of different stations including dumb-bell push-up rows, inverted rows and ab rollouts.*

**B**ronze

**2.** Plan a 10-station circuit to improve muscular endurance.

## Core stability training

Core stability describes your capacity to control the muscles that maintain stability around your lower back, pelvis, and abdomen. Your abdominal muscles (including your rectus abdominis, your internal obliques, and your external obliques) combine with the muscles in your lower back to help support the area and prevent unwanted movement. Poor core stability is often characterized by lower back pain.

Good core stability is essential for all sports and physical activities because the core muscles are involved in most movements, and when the core muscles are strong they create a stable base from which these movements can be performed powerfully. They can also be performed with control and, in this way, good core stability also helps to prevent injury.

Core stability training involves exercises that strengthen the muscles of the core. These include:

➜ *Good core stability enables a discus thrower to create a strong, powerful, and controlled rotation.*

➜ *The plank*

➜ *The bridge*

➜ *The bird dog*

Pilates is a form of core stability training.

| Advantages of core stability training | Disadvantages of core stability training |
|---|---|
| • Can be done anywhere.<br>• Does not require a lot of space.<br>• Does not require a lot of expensive equipment.<br>• Benefits all performers.<br>• Does not require long training sessions. | • Performers need to learn the correct technique for each exercise to prevent injury.<br>• Fitness classes, like Pilates, tend to take place at sports centres or gyms, and can be expensive to attend.<br>• Can be tedious, because it may not get the heart beating as fast as other methods of training. |

### B ronze

**3.** Take part in a core stability training session. Can you add any more advantages and disadvantages to the lists?

# Training methods to improve flexibility

## Static stretching

There are two main types of static stretches: active stretches and passive stretches. Active stretches involve the performer applying the force that lengthens and stretches the muscles. Passive stretches involve a partner, wall, barre, or other object assisting the performer with the stretch.

It is important that the muscles that will be used most by the performer are stretched. For example, an outfield player in a hockey team might focus on stretching their hamstrings, quadriceps, and gastrocnemius, while the goalkeeper in the same team might spend more time stretching their deltoids and both latissimi dorsi. This is because the different positions place demands on different muscles.

→ *This dancer is using a barre to help him stretch his hamstrings, using a passive static stretch.*

External obliques

Deltoids

Abdominals

Biceps

Gastrocnemius

Triceps

Adductors

Hamstrings

Hip flexor

Gluteus maximus

Torso

Quadriceps

Erector spinae

Hamstrings

→ *An artwork showing a selection of the most commonly performed active static stretches.*

| Advantages of static stretching | Disadvantages of static stretching |
| --- | --- |
| • Can be done anywhere.<br>• Does not require a lot of space.<br>• Does not require any expensive equipment.<br>• Benefits all performers.<br>• Can be adjusted to suit the needs of the performer. | • Performers need to learn the correct technique for each exercise to prevent injury.<br>• Can be tedious, especially if the performer would prefer to be playing sport. |

## Dynamic stretching

Dynamic stretches are movements that bring about a stretch but do not involve holding the muscle in a static position. They often mimic sporting movements. Dynamic stretches include the lunge and the cat cow stretch:

| Advantages of dynamic stretching | Disadvantages of dynamic stretching |
|---|---|
| • Can be done anywhere at any time.<br>• Does not require a lot of space.<br>• Does not require any expensive equipment.<br>• Benefits all performers.<br>• Can be adjusted to suit the needs of the performer.<br>• Increases mobility as well as flexibility. | • Performers need to learn the correct technique for each exercise to prevent injury.<br>• Comes with a higher risk of injury than static stretching.<br>• Can be tedious, especially if the performer would prefer to be playing sport. |

→ *The cat cow stretch*

## Proprioceptive neuromuscular facilitation (PNF) stretching

With PNF stretching, the performer has help from a partner or uses an immovable object to provide resistance, to push the limb and stretch the muscles further than the performer can stretch them on their own.

The muscle is first stretched for about six seconds, with the partner or the immovable object inhibiting movement. The muscle is relaxed for a brief moment, before the partner or the immovable object stretches the muscle further using a passive static stretch for 20–30 seconds.

| Advantages of PNF stretching | Disadvantages of PNF stretching |
|---|---|
| • Can be done anywhere at any time.<br>• Does not require a lot of space.<br>• Does not require any expensive equipment.<br>• Benefits all performers.<br>• Can be adjusted to suit the needs of the performer.<br>• Very effective as part of a rehabilitation programme. | • Must only be performed after muscles are fully warmed up.<br>• Best performed with a partner who is fully trained.<br>• There is a risk of injury if not performed correctly.<br>• Can be tedious, especially if the performer would prefer to be playing sport. |

### B ronze/Silver

4.  a) Choose your favourite sport or physical activity. Fold a piece of A4 paper in half three times to create eight small boxes. In each box, draw a diagram of a static stretch or a dynamic stretch that is suitable for your chosen sport or physical activity. Make sure you include stretches for the upper body and the lower body.

    b) Explain how a performer taking part in your chosen sport or physical activity would benefit from the stretches you have drawn.

    c) Are there any disadvantages to the stretches you have drawn or to static stretching or dynamic stretching in general for a performer taking part in your chosen sport or physical activity?

## Training methods to improve speed

### Interval training

Interval training can be used to develop speed. The intervals should be shorter and performed at a higher intensity – as close to maximum intensity as possible – than they are if interval training is being used to develop aerobic endurance. The number of recovery periods and the length of the recovery periods should also be increased to compensate for the shorter and higher-intensity work periods.

### Sprint training

Sprint training is a form of interval training. The performer increases their running speed from jogging to striding and finally to sprinting at maximum pace. Each change of pace usually takes place every 50 metres. This is usually repeated about five times, with 50 metres of walking in between, before a longer, 10-minute rest period.

### Sport-specific speed training

Sport-specific speed training is also known as Speed, Agility and Quickness (SAQ®) training. It aims to improve how quickly a performer moves their limbs, how quickly they are able to change direction, and how quickly they are able to respond to stimuli, and is focused on the demands of the performer's specific sport.

For example, travelling through ladders and hurdles and changing direction at pace mimic the movements football players make on the pitch. Moving your feet quickly over small distances replicates the start of a sprint towards the ball and changing direction replicates the movements required when marking an opponent.

> **S ilver**
>
> 5.  a) Choose a sport you know well and design a sport-specific speed training session for that sport.
>
>     b) Explain how the drills you have chosen to include in your training session are specific to your chosen sport.

| Advantages of interval training for improving speed | Disadvantages of interval training for improving speed |
|---|---|
| • Does not require expensive equipment.<br>• Does not require long training sessions.<br>• Flexible, so can be adjusted to suit the needs of the performer. | • Performers need to be motivated to tolerate the discomfort of the high-intensity work periods.<br>• Longer recovery time between training sessions is needed.<br>• There is a higher risk of injury because of the repeated use of maximal-intensity movements. |

| Advantages of sprint training | Disadvantages of sprint training |
|---|---|
| • Does not require expensive equipment.<br>• Does not require long training sessions.<br>• Flexible, so can be adjusted to suit the needs of the performer. | • Performers need to be motivated to tolerate the discomfort of the high-intensity work periods.<br>• Longer recovery time between training sessions is needed.<br>• There is a higher risk of injury because of the repeated use of maximal-intensity movements.<br>• Only relevant to sports where sprinting is a key component. |

| Advantages of sport-specific speed training | Disadvantages of sport-specific speed training |
|---|---|
| • Relatively straightforward to carry out.<br>• Does not require long training sessions.<br>• Designed specifically to suit the needs of the performer and their sport. | • A coach is required to design a training programme.<br>• Performers need to be motivated to tolerate the discomfort of the high-intensity work periods.<br>• Longer recovery time between training sessions is needed.<br>• SAQ® equipment can be expensive. |

# Training methods to improve strength

Weight training to improve strength involves using free weights or resistance machines to bring about hypertrophy.

 **Link**

Look back at page 16 to remind yourself about hypertrophy.

Each time a performer completes a lifting or moving action they are working against resistance (the amount of force or weight that must be lifted or moved). Each lift or movement is known as a repetition or 'rep', and 'one repetition maximum' or '1RM' is the maximum weight a person can lift or move in a single repetition of the exercise. The number of repetitions a performer completes without a rest is called a 'set' and there should be a rest period between sets.

People who are training to improve their strength should lift 70 per cent of their 1RM. They should perform three sets of six reps of each exercise, with one-minute intervals of rest between each set.

## Free weights

Free weights include dumb-bells, barbells, and kettlebells.

| Advantages of free weights | Disadvantages of free weights |
|---|---|
| • Develops core stability alongside developing strength in the specific muscles trained, because the performer has to stabilize their body and avoid unwanted movements while lifting the weights.<br>• Very flexible, so can be designed to meet the specific needs of the performer.<br>• Lots of variety, so it is more interesting than many other types of training. | • Requires expensive equipment.<br>• Usually needs to be carried out at a gym, which can be expensive to access.<br>• Not appropriate for beginners.<br>• Good technique is essential because poor technique can lead to injury.<br>• Should be performed with a partner, a 'spotter'.<br>• Adequate rest is required between training sessions, to allow the muscles trained time to recover and repair. |

## Resistance machines

Resistance machines include the lat pull down machine, which develops the latissimus dorsi muscles along with other upper-body muscles, and the leg press machine, which develops the muscles in the legs including the hamstrings and the quadriceps.

| Advantages of resistance machines | Disadvantages of resistance machines |
|---|---|
| • Good for beginners because the machine promotes good technique.<br>• Very flexible, so can be designed to meet the specific needs of the performer.<br>• Can be carried out alone. | • Requires expensive equipment.<br>• Usually needs to be carried out at a gym, which can be expensive to access.<br>• Limited development of core stability.<br>• Adequate rest is required between training sessions, to allow the muscles trained time to recover and repair. |

**G old**

6. Martha is a 65-year-old woman who has not exercised for many years. Her doctor is encouraging her to get fit. In particular, she has been urged to improve her strength. Evaluate which method of training to improve strength would be more appropriate for Martha.

Remember, when you evaluate something, you need to bring together all the information you have about a topic and review it before reaching a conclusion.

## Training methods to improve power

### Plyometrics

Plyometrics involves the use of high-impact jumping, bounding, and hopping exercises to train muscles to contract more powerfully. A muscle is lengthened, often achieved through a landing, before being contracted, often achieved by leaving the ground again. It is the performer's ability to produce a strong contraction quickly that results in power, because power is the ability to combine strength and speed.

Examples of plyometric exercises include the following:

→ *A box jump*

→ *A clap press-up*

→ *A barrier jump*

| Advantages of plyometrics | Disadvantages of plyometrics |
|---|---|
| • Mimics sporting action.<br>• Requires minimal equipment, which is easy to set up.<br>• Can easily be added to a circuit training session. | • Not suitable for beginners because a good level of strength is required before doing plyometric exercises.<br>• High-impact exercises can cause stress to joints.<br>• Adequate rest is required between training sessions, to allow the muscles trained time to recover and develop. |

### Anaerobic hill sprints

An anaerobic hill sprint is a sprint lasting no more than 30 seconds up a hill with a gradient of 5–15 degrees. The sprint is followed by a slow jog or a walk down the hill, taking 60–90 seconds, to allow the performer to recover. The performer's running technique should involve a vigorous arm drive and a high knee lift, and they should look straight ahead and not at their feet, so they are running upright and not leaning forwards. Depending on their level of fitness, a performer should complete 10–20 anaerobic hill sprints in a training session.

This is what a gradient of 5–15 degrees looks like:

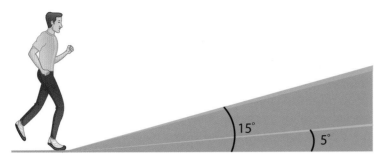

| Advantages of anaerobic hill sprints | Disadvantages of anaerobic hill sprints |
|---|---|
| • Improve the body's ability to delay, and then cope with, the accumulation of lactic acid.<br>• Improve strength and speed, as well as power.<br>• Increase resistance to injury as muscles and connective tissues adapt to the stress placed on them. | • A hill of the suitable gradient is required.<br>• Not suitable for beginners because a good level of strength and muscular endurance is required before doing anaerobic hill sprints.<br>• Adequate rest is required between training sessions, to allow the muscles trained time to recover and develop.<br>• May not be appropriate in wet or icy weather because of the increased risk of falling over and sustaining an injury. |

## CrossFit®

CrossFit® is a group fitness programme designed by Greg Glassman. It takes exercises from a range of different disciplines, including plyometrics, weightlifting, and aerobics, and weaves them together into a high-intensity training programme that is constantly changing.

| Advantages of CrossFit® | Disadvantages of CrossFit® |
|---|---|
| • Improves cardiovascular endurance and muscular endurance, as well as strength, speed, and power.<br>• Training with other people is very motivating.<br>• Very varied, so it does not become tedious. | • It is easy to focus on performing as many repetitions of an exercise as possible in as short a time as possible and forget about performing the exercises properly and developing strength alongside speed. This can lead to injury.<br>• Performers need to be motivated to tolerate the discomfort of the high-intensity work periods.<br>• Performers need to learn the correct technique for each exercise to prevent injury.<br>• Adequate rest is required between training sessions, to allow the muscles trained time to recover and develop.<br>• You have to join a CrossFit® gym to take part in CrossFit® training, which can be expensive. |

### G old

7. Tom is 19 years old and is a triathlete. He is placing fourth and fifth in competitions and his coach thinks that increasing his power will help him place higher in future competitions. Evaluate which method of training to improve power would be most appropriate for Tom.

The principles of training and the FITT principles are relevant to everyone who takes part in sport and physical activity, from the complete beginner to the elite performer. You must apply the **principles of training** to make progress during a training programme. The principles of training ensure that training is effective and leads to the adaptations that bring about improvements in performance. Applying the **FITT principles** to a training programme ensures that training is optimized for success. FITT stands for Frequency, Intensity, Type, and Time.

 **Link**

Remind yourself about the positive adaptations that take place as a result of taking part in sport and physical activity on pages 14–17.

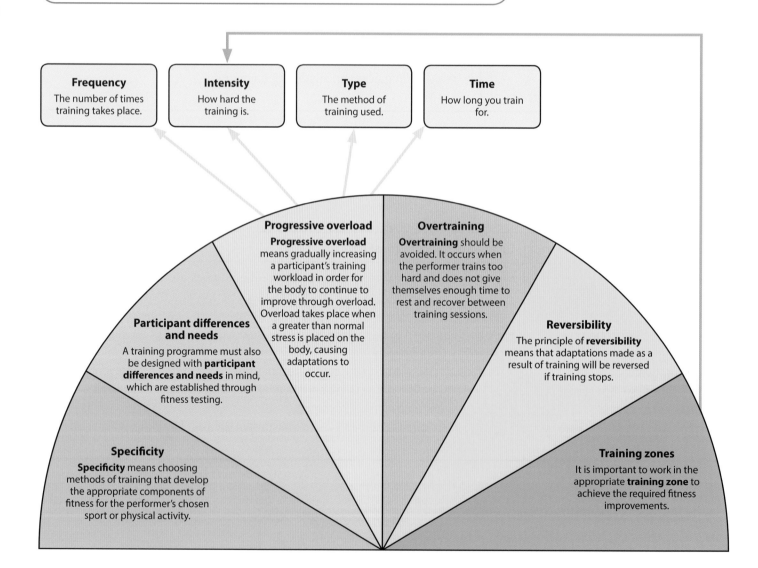

**Frequency**
The number of times training takes place.

**Intensity**
How hard the training is.

**Type**
The method of training used.

**Time**
How long you train for.

**Progressive overload**
Progressive overload means gradually increasing a participant's training workload in order for the body to continue to improve through overload. Overload takes place when a greater than normal stress is placed on the body, causing adaptations to occur.

**Overtraining**
**Overtraining** should be avoided. It occurs when the performer trains too hard and does not give themselves enough time to rest and recover between training sessions.

**Participant differences and needs**
A training programme must also be designed with **participant differences and needs** in mind, which are established through fitness testing.

**Reversibility**
The principle of **reversibility** means that adaptations made as a result of training will be reversed if training stops.

**Specificity**
**Specificity** means choosing methods of training that develop the appropriate components of fitness for the performer's chosen sport or physical activity.

**Training zones**
It is important to work in the appropriate **training zone** to achieve the required fitness improvements.

# Specificity

In order for a training programme to be effective it must be specifically designed with the performer's chosen sport or physical activity in mind. It must apply the principle of specificity.

To achieve adaptations that help the performer to succeed in their chosen sporting goals, the performer must train their body to be better at the things specifically required by the sport or physical activity they want to excel at. They must train to improve the appropriate components of fitness and the appropriate muscle groups.

As a result, it should come as no surprise that swimmers will do a lot of their training in the pool and cyclists will do a lot of their training on a bike. It will also be no surprise that endurance swimmers will swim further in training than sprint swimmers, while sprint cyclists will train more powerfully than endurance cyclists.

## B ronze

1.  How would the following sports performers apply the principle of specificity in their training? Think about the components of fitness they need in order to compete successfully and the key muscle groups they use. You may wish to do some research on the internet.

→ *Tirunesh Dibaba: 10,000m runner*

→ *Jason Kenny: sprint cyclist*

→ *Duncan Scott: 100m and 200m freestyle swimmer*

## Participant differences and needs

A training programme for a beginner will be very different from a training programme for an elite performer, and a training programme for a beginner aged 30 will be very different from a training programme for a beginner aged 75. A successful training programme must be designed with a participant's individual needs in mind.

Fitness testing will establish a participant's strengths and weaknesses in the components of fitness that are important for the sport or physical activity that they want to take part in. The training programme can then be designed to improve their weaknesses and build on their strengths.

**B** ronze/Silver

2.  Saoirse plays tennis and she has asked you to devise a training programme to help her improve her game. You have identified the three most important components of fitness for a tennis player as aerobic endurance, speed, and muscular endurance, and asked Saoirse to complete some fitness testing. Her scores are as follows:

    - 30-metre sprint test: above average
    - Cooper 12-minute run test: average
    - one-minute sit-up test: below average.

    a) Based on her fitness test results, which component of fitness should Saoirse's training focus on? Explain why.

    b) What sort of activities should Saoirse include in her training programme?

# Progressive overload

To be effective, training should get harder as the weeks go by and as the body adapts. This is the principle of progressive overload. If a performer sticks to the same training plan for a long period of time, their level of fitness will plateau and no further improvements will take place. The body needs to be exposed to progressively more challenging training in order to continue to adapt.

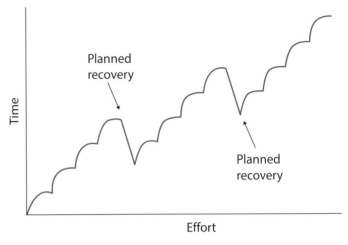

→ *Applying the principle of progressive overload ensures the body continues to develop and the training programme produces the desired results.*

The FITT principles ensure that a training programme incorporates progressive overload.

 **Frequency**

This is the number of times training takes place.

Gradually increasing the number of training sessions each week achieves progressive overload. However, it is important to remember that adaptation occurs during periods of rest and recovery, therefore it is important to incorporate rest days into a training programme.

How often a person should train will depend on their current fitness levels. A beginner should start by training a couple of times a week, increasing the frequency of training sessions as time passes and they get fitter. A more experienced performer will train more frequently. Many experienced performers alternate the areas of the body that they train each day, to allow time for recovery, and build in at least one day each week when they do not train at all. This is because training too frequently is one cause of overtraining, which can lead to injury.

#  **I ntensity**

This is how hard the training is.

Training harder over time achieves progressive overload. Raising the intensity of a training session may mean that the training time needs to be reduced to avoid overtraining.

The appropriate intensity for a training session will vary according to the participant's individual needs. What represents an intense workout for a beginner will fall well below an elite performer's requirements. It is, therefore, important to measure how hard the performer is working throughout a training session and to tailor the activities accordingly.

One of the most effective ways to measure intensity is to calculate your training zones and then measure your heart rate or calculate your Rate of Perceived Exertion (RPE) during exercise to ensure you are working within the correct training zone.

## Training zones

The training zones can be represented as a pyramid:

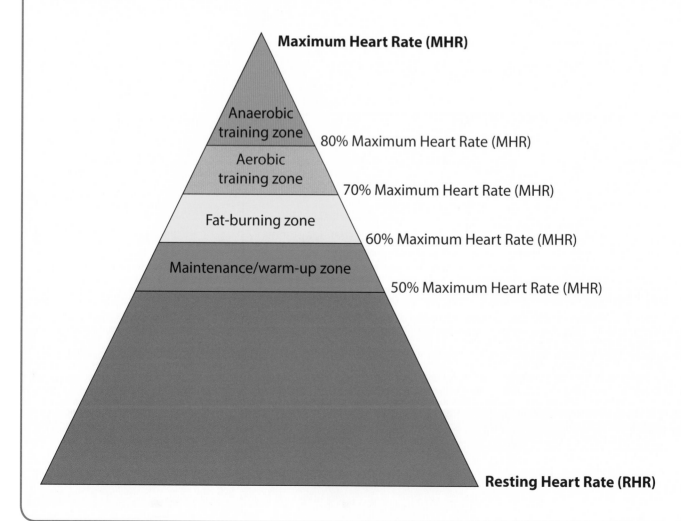

Your Maximum Heart Rate (MHR) is calculated using a simple formula:

MHR = 220 − age

This means that the Maximum Heart Rate and training zones for a 15 year old are as follows:

MHR = 220 − 15 = 205 beats per minute

Anaerobic training zone = 80–100% of MHR
80% × 205 = 164
100% × 205 = 205
Anaerobic training zone = 164–205 beats per minute

Aerobic training zone = 70–80% of MHR
70% × 205 = 143.5, rounded up to 144
80% × 205 = 164
Aerobic training zone = 144–164 beats per minute

Fat-burning zone = 60–70% of MHR
60% × 205 = 123
70% × 205 = 143.5, rounded up to 144
Fat-burning zone = 123–144 beats per minute

Maintenance/warm-up zone = 50–60% of MHR
50% × 205 = 102.5, rounded up to 103
60% × 205 = 123
Maintenance/warm-up zone = 103–123 beats per minute

This means that a 15 year old should work hard enough to make their heart contract between 144 and 164 times per minute to work in the aerobic training zone.

## Measuring your heart rate

You can measure your heart rate using a heart rate monitor or by hand:

→ *When the heart beats it emits an electrical signal. Heart rate monitors count the number of electrical signals emitted over one minute. One electrical signal is one beat of the heart. Today, many smartwatches contain heart rate monitors, and the data are collected in an app.*

➡ *When the heart beats it causes a wave of pressure as blood is forced through the arteries. This can be felt as a pulse at points throughout the body, including the wrist (the radial pulse) and the neck (the carotid pulse). You can take your pulse at the radial pulse by placing the index and middle finger of one hand on the inside of the wrist of the other hand, in the soft area between the bone and the tendon near the base of the thumb. You can take your pulse at the carotid pulse by placing the index and middle finger of one hand on your neck, to the side of your trachea. If you struggle to find your pulse, try moving your fingers around or pressing a little harder. Count how many beats you can feel in 15 seconds and multiply the answer by four to get your heart rate.*

## Calculating your Rate of Perceived Exertion (RPE)

The Rate of Perceived Exertion (RPE) scale is used to measure exercise intensity by asking a performer to rate their perceived level of exertion. There are a number of RPE scales in existence, but the most common is the 15-point scale shown here:

| RPE | Effort |
|-----|--------|
| 6 | 20% effort |
| 7 | 30% effort: very, very light intensity |
| 8 | 40% effort |
| 9 | 50% effort: very light intensity |
| 10 | 55% effort |
| 11 | 60% effort: fairly light intensity |
| 12 | 65% effort |
| 13 | 70% effort: somewhat hard intensity |
| 14 | 75% effort |
| 15 | 80% effort: hard intensity |
| 16 | 85% effort |
| 17 | 90% effort: very hard intensity |
| 18 | 95% effort |
| 19 | 100% effort: very, very hard intensity |
| 20 | Exhaustion |

## Working at the correct intensity

The importance of knowing how hard you are working can best be seen when comparing continuous training and interval training. Each method of training requires you to work differently with intensity.

Continuous training involves performing an activity at a steady intensity in the aerobic training zone:

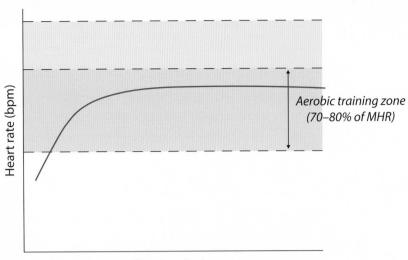

Interval training involves predetermined periods of work in the anaerobic training zone and periods of rest in the aerobic training zone:

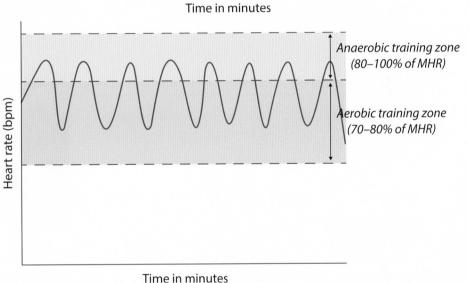

**3.** Christopher is 24 years old. Here are the data collected from his smartwatch during a recent interval training session.

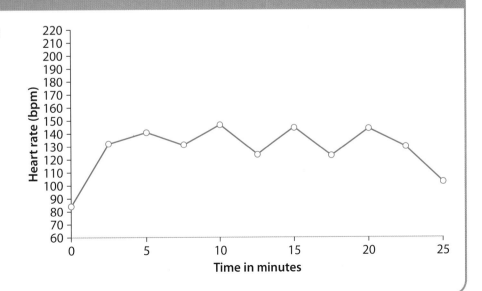

**a)** Is Christopher working at the appropriate intensity?

**b)** Explain your answer.

# ype

This is the method of training used.

Changing the type of training used gives the body's systems a fresh challenge, thereby achieving progressive overload. This could involve moving from continuous training to interval training or it could involve introducing plyometric exercises into your weight training programme.

Changing the type of training, or adding additional types of training to a training programme, enables a performer to develop more than one component of fitness at the same time. For example, someone new to exercise might begin by developing their aerobic endurance with continuous training but, after a time, may introduce a session in the gym on the resistance machines so that they can work on improving their strength.

Including a variety of training methods in a training programme can also help ensure it does not get tedious. It is a good idea to mix things up, training in the gym and outside, and working on improving specific components of fitness and sport-specific skills and techniques.

➜ *Footballers train in the gym and on the pitch.*

# ime

This is how long you train for.

Increasing, over time, the length of your runs or swims, the number of repetitions during a weight training session, or the number of circuits in a circuit training session delivers progressive overload.

The length of time a performer should train for to achieve progressive overload will depend on the method of training chosen, the component of fitness being trained, and the performer's fitness test results. For example:

- High-intensity methods of training, such as plyometrics and anaerobic hill sprints, should only be carried out for a short period of time, but increasing the number of repetitions gradually over time will provide progressive overload.
- A performer who wants to lose weight should work for at least 28 minutes in the fat-burning zone, whereas a performer training to improve their aerobic endurance should work for at least 20 minutes in the aerobic training zone. Both should gradually add time to their workouts to achieve progressive overload.
- A performer training to improve muscular endurance should lift lower weights for a higher number of repetitions, whereas a performer training to improve strength should lift higher weights for a lower number of repetitions.

## Overtraining

Overtraining occurs when the intensity of exercise exceeds the body's ability to recover, such as when a performer increases their training workload too quickly. A performer who has overtrained will cease to make progress and can even begin to lose strength and fitness. They are also more likely to injure themselves.

So how much is too much? Your level of fitness and the type of training you are doing influence how much is too much. Applying the principle of progressive overload and giving your body time to rest and recover between training sessions will help you to avoid overtraining.

## Reversibility

Training adaptations are only temporary. If training stops or reduces in intensity, the gains that have been achieved will be lost relatively quickly. Fitness developments will, in essence, reverse. This is sometimes referred to as de-training.

Situations in which performers will experience reversibility include:

- when they cannot train because of illness or an injury
- when they do not train regularly enough
- when they do not train effectively
- during the off-season
- when they prioritize another component of fitness; for example, speed may reduce if a performer focuses on improving their aerobic endurance for an extended period of time.

Knowing about reversibility is important for two reasons. Firstly, knowing about it means you can make sure it does not happen as a result of poor motivation or poor planning. Secondly, if you are injured, you will understand the importance of giving yourself time after rehabilitation to build back to your previous levels of fitness. Returning to challenging training too soon after an injury is likely to slow your recovery or cause you to re-injure yourself.

## B ronze

4. Billy Vunipola of Saracens and England had to pull out of the British and Irish Lions summer tour to New Zealand because of a shoulder injury. As the Lions tour only happens every four years, and the competition to be selected is fierce, this must have been a difficult time for him.

   a) What training advice would you have given Billy to reduce the effects of reversibility during the summer of 2017 while his shoulder healed?

   b) Following his shoulder rehabilitation, what would Billy have needed to consider as he prepared for the 2017/2018 season?

When you are planning a fitness training programme, it is essential to gather information about the performer and to work with them to develop a training programme that meets their needs. Every performer has different goals, different fitness levels, and different likes and dislikes, and a training programme that takes all these into account is much more likely to be successful.

There are three steps to designing an effective fitness training programme.

## Step 1: Using a person-centred approach

Start by finding out as much as you can about the person for whom you are designing the training programme.

### Likes and dislikes

How the performer feels about a fitness programme will play a large part in how they approach it and, ultimately, how successful it is. It is, therefore, important to understand what they like and what they dislike. If they absolutely hate swimming, it is probably not a good idea to include a weekly swim in their fitness programme. But, on the other hand, if they tell you that they really like running, you can choose methods of training that have a focus on running.

### Availability to exercise

Finding out how much time a performer has to exercise is fundamental to developing a fitness programme they will be able to stick to. Expecting a single working parent to commit to training four nights a week is probably unrealistic, but they might be able to train for several hours on a Saturday morning while someone else takes care of their children.

### Medical history

It is important to find out if the performer has any medical issues or lifestyle choices that need to be considered, so performers should always complete a health-screening questionnaire like a Physical Activity Readiness Questionnaire (PAR-Q) before embarking on a fitness programme. For example, a programme for a performer who suffers from back pain should not include a lot of high-impact activities.

### Goal

The most common fitness goal is to lose weight but goals may also be more specific, for example, to complete a 10K run in 60 minutes or without stopping and walking. The more specific a goal, the better able a performer is to measure their progress towards their goal and the more motivated they are likely to be to stick to their fitness programme.

## Step 2: Establishing the aims and objectives of the training programme

It is important to establish the aims and objectives of the training programme before you delve into the detail. Having clear aims and objectives helps you ensure that the training programme you are designing will support the performer to meet their goal. Ask yourself: What do I want the performer to be able to do at the end of the training programme that they could not do at the start? Your aims are what you want to achieve with the training programme. Your objectives are the steps you are going to take to achieve your aims.

A central part of establishing aims and objectives is deciding which components of fitness the performer requires a high level of fitness in, in order to reach their goal. Measuring the performer's level of fitness in these components of fitness will then indicate what the training programme should focus on and how much improvement is required to meet the performer's goal.

The aims and objectives for a training programme for someone who wants to run a 10K in 60 minutes might be as follows:

- Aims: To improve aerobic endurance and muscular endurance to such an extent that the performer can run a 10K in 60 minutes in six weeks' time.
- Objectives: By the end of the training programme, the performer will be able to run 2000 metres, up from 1700 metres, in the Cooper 12-minute run test and perform 36 sit-ups, up from 29 sit-ups, in the one-minute sit-up test.

The more specific you can be with your aims and objectives, the easier it is to plan a training programme that delivers them.

## Step 3: Designing a safe and effective training programme

Use the information you have about the performer and your aims and objectives to choose the most appropriate methods of training. Then apply the principles of training and the FITT principles to design a safe and effective training programme.

A training programme will contain a series of training sessions. Each training session should consist of:

- **a warm-up**, to prepare the mind and body for the activity ahead. A warm-up increases heart rate and joint mobility, reduces the risk of injury, and helps to improve performance.
- **the main component**, focusing on the chosen method of training.
- **a cool-down**, to help the performer's body systems gradually return to their pre-exercise state. A cool-down gradually decreases heart rate and encourages the removal of waste products, including lactic acid, thereby reducing the risk of muscle soreness in the days following the training session.

A training programme usually lasts about six weeks and, at the end of the training programme, it is important to review the aims of the programme and decide whether or not they have been met. If the goals have been met, then a new training programme, with new aims and objectives, can be set to ensure the performer continues to improve. If the aims have not been met, then it can be extremely beneficial to evaluate why this was the case; the insights gained can inform the planning of future training programmes.

> **⊘ Link**
>
> You can find out more about the activities that make for good warm-ups and good cool-downs on pages 137 and 140.

**B** ronze/Silver

1. Ethan is an experienced runner who has completed several half marathons and wants to run in his first marathon in six weeks' time. He is worried about running 26.2 miles rather than the 13.1 miles he is used to and has asked for some advice.

   a) Look at Ethan's six-week training programme and comment on how well he has used the principles of training and the FITT principles.

   b) Explain how Ethan could improve his training programme, using the principles of training and the FITT principles, to better prepare him for his upcoming marathon.

Week 1, Week 2, and Week 3:

| Monday | Tuesday | Wednesday | Thursday | Friday | Saturday | Sunday |
|---|---|---|---|---|---|---|
| Warm-up<br><br>1 hour continuous training, running at RPE 12<br><br>Cool-down | Rest | Warm-up<br><br>45 minutes interval training, running at RPE 12<br><br>Cool-down | Rest | Warm-up<br><br>1 hour continuous training, running at RPE 12<br><br>Cool-down | Rest | Warm-up<br><br>45 minutes interval training, running at RPE 12<br><br>Cool-down |

Week 4, Week 5, and Week 6:

| Monday | Tuesday | Wednesday | Thursday | Friday | Saturday | Sunday |
|---|---|---|---|---|---|---|
| Warm-up<br><br>1.5 hours continuous training, running at RPE 12<br><br>Cool-down | Rest | Warm-up<br><br>1 hour interval training, running at RPE 12<br><br>Cool-down | Rest | Warm-up<br><br>1.5 hours continuous training, running at RPE 12<br><br>Cool-down | Rest | Warm-up<br><br>1 hour interval training, running at RPE 12<br><br>Cool-down |

 **G** old

2. Read Abi's profile and design a six-week training programme for her.

   > Abi is 22 years old and healthy. She enjoys being active but doesn't like competitive sport. She is happy swimming but would like to try running because she has moved near to a big park where lots of people run and she thinks it would be fun to join them.
   >
   > Abi works in an office during the week, so is free to exercise in the evenings and at weekends. She is not an early riser, so hates the idea of exercising before work.
   >
   > She would like to meet people, because she has just moved to the area, and would like to keep fit because she has just started working in an office and realizes she could put on quite a bit of weight if she doesn't keep active.

The nutrients that the body needs are classified as **macronutrients**, which you need to eat in large quantities, and **micronutrients**, which you need to consume in smaller quantities. Carbohydrates, proteins, and fats are all macronutrients and each has a special role in keeping us healthy and enabling us to participate in sport and physical activity.

## Carbohydrates

**Carbohydrates** are the body's main source of energy. They are stored in the body as glycogen, which is broken down into glucose by the liver to provide the body with energy when it needs it. In this way, carbohydrates provide fuel for muscle contractions, enabling us to carry out everyday activities like walking to school and enabling us to take part in sport and physical activity. Glucose, derived from carbohydrates, is also essential for good brain function; it is hard to think clearly when you are hungry and your body is low on glucose as a result.

There are two types of carbohydrate:

1. **Simple carbohydrates**, also known as simple sugars, break down into glucose quickly, providing a quick burst of energy. For this reason, it can be beneficial to consume simple carbohydrates if you are feeling tired before, during, or after exercise.

➜ *Simple carbohydrates are found in sweets, honey, fruit and fruit juice, chocolate, as well as many snacks and glucose energy drinks.*

2. **Complex carbohydrates** break down into glucose slowly, releasing energy over a much longer period of time than simple carbohydrates. This makes them very important for endurance performers working aerobically and pasta and rice will be staples of an endurance performer's diet.

➜ *Complex carbohydrates are found in many different foods, including pasta, rice, bread, cereals, oats, and potatoes. It is better to eat wholegrain versions of these foods because they contain fibre.* **Fibre** *helps your body absorb vital nutrients and remove waste products by providing the bulk that is needed to move them through your digestive system. Fibre can also be found in vegetables.*

## Protein

**Protein** provides the body with amino acids. Amino acids are the building blocks of all human cells, controlling many vital processes, and they are essential for muscle growth and repair. As a result, they play an important role in promoting hypertrophy, helping to make your muscles bigger and stronger, and minimizing your risk of injury.

The body requires 22 different amino acids. Eight of these are called '**essential amino acids**'. This is because they have to be supplied by the food you eat; your body cannot make them itself. The remaining 14 amino acids, called '**non-essential amino acids**', can be made by the body. The terms 'essential amino acids' and 'non-essential amino acids' do not mean that non-essential amino acids are less important, just that the body can make them; all 22 amino acids are vital for a healthy body.

→ *Chicken, turkey, lean beef, fish, eggs, beans, nuts, seeds, and non-meat protein substitutes such as Quorn™ are all good sources of protein.*

 **Link**

Turn back to page 16 to remind yourself about hypertrophy.

## Fats

**Fats** are an essential part of a healthy diet. Consuming fats does not make you fat; it is consuming more calories than you burn that makes you gain weight. Fats are an important source of energy. They are also important for transporting fat-soluble vitamins around the body, and certain fatty acids are vital for good health.

There are two main types of fat:

1. **Saturated fats** are typically solid at room temperature. Too much saturated fat in a diet increases the total amount of cholesterol in your blood, increasing your risk of coronary heart disease, so foods containing saturated fats should be limited.

→ *Saturated fats are found in fatty meat, cheese, and butter, as well as cakes, crisps, and biscuits.*

2. **Unsaturated fats** are normally liquid at room temperature. They are much healthier for you than saturated fats, and play a role in reducing your risk of developing coronary heart disease. They are also the body's second source of energy, after carbohydrates. Unsaturated fat is a very good source of energy but it takes a relatively long time to convert fat into energy. This can be useful if you are involved in high-level endurance training, but someone who has a high-fat diet and does not train hard will put on weight.

→ *Oily fish, avocados, almonds, walnuts, and pumpkin seeds are all good sources of unsaturated fats, as are oils such as olive oil.*

Vitamins and minerals are micronutrients. Vitamins play an important role in ensuring that vital chemical reactions take place in the body and minerals play an essential role in almost all bodily functions. Some of the most important vitamins and minerals, and their main benefits to the body, are discussed below.

## Vitamin A

Vitamin A is important for eye health. It therefore plays a vital role in hand–eye coordination (your hands and eyes working together to do things that require speed and accuracy, such as catching a ball) and positional awareness (knowing where you are in relation to other people or other objects, such as another player or a ball), both of which rely on good eyesight.

➜ *Mackerel is a good source of vitamin A, as are beef and chicken liver and dairy products such as milk, cheese, and eggs. Vitamin A can also be found in a wide range of vegetables, including kale and carrots.*

## Vitamin B1

Vitamin B1, also known as thiamine, is essential for energy production because it plays an important role in breaking down the carbohydrates we eat into energy. Consequently, endurance performers who consume a lot of carbohydrates to provide them with the energy to keep going for longer, also need to make sure they are eating enough foods rich in vitamin B1.

➜ *Red kidney beans are a good source of vitamin B1, as are wholegrain rice, bran, pork, and beef, as well as peas and other beans, including soya beans and mung beans.*

## Vitamin C

Vitamin C is critical for maintaining a healthy, functioning immune system. The immune system is our body's defence against bacteria, viruses, and other microorganisms that can cause disease, so vitamin C helps prevent illness. This means we can keep on doing what we want and need to do, including training and competing for a sports performer.

➜ *Kale is a great source of vitamin C, as is most other fresh fruit and vegetables, including oranges, strawberries, green peppers, and Brussels sprouts.*

## Vitamin D

Vitamin D is crucial for healthy bones and teeth, which all sports performers need, and it also plays a role in keeping muscles strong and healthy. It is produced in your body when your skin is exposed to sunlight, but there are also dietary sources of vitamin D and people who are not regularly exposed to sunlight are encouraged to take vitamin D supplements.

➜ *Egg yolks are a dietary source of vitamin D. It can also be found in oily fish, red meat, liver, and fortified foods such as fortified cereals.*

## Potassium

Potassium is an electrolyte. Electrolytes are substances that conduct electricity when dissolved in water and they play a vital role in enabling muscles and nerves to function. Potassium is particularly important for keeping the fluids in the body in balance. You lose potassium when you sweat, so it is important to replenish your body with potassium during and after high-intensity exercise so that your cells remain hydrated.

→ *Bananas are a good source of potassium, as are sunflower seeds, potatoes, and yoghurt. Many sports drinks contain added electrolytes, including potassium.*

## Iron

Iron is found in red blood cells and plays a critical role in enabling them to carry oxygen around the body. It also plays a part in the creation of new red blood cells. Consequently, iron increases your ability to work aerobically because it increases the efficiency with which oxygen is carried to your working muscles and organs and carbon dioxide is carried away from them.

→ *Cashew nuts are a good source of iron. Iron can also be found in liver, beef, turkey, eggs, kidney beans, and spinach.*

## Calcium

Calcium is crucial for strong, healthy bones. Everyone benefits from strong, healthy bones, but they are particularly important for people involved in contact sports or high-impact physical activities who are most at risk from fractures.

→ *Milk contains calcium, as do other dairy products such as cheddar cheese, as well as wholegrains and green leafy vegetables.*

## B ronze

1.  Design three main evening meals containing the three macronutrients (carbohydrates, protein, and fats) and the seven micronutrients (vitamin A, vitamin B1, vitamin C, vitamin D, potassium, iron, and calcium) discussed.

    **a)** One meal should be designed for someone who eats meat, fish, and dairy products.

    **b)** One meal should be designed for a vegetarian (someone who does not eat meat or fish).

    **c)** One meal should be designed for a vegan (someone who does not eat meat, fish, or dairy products).

    When you're designing your meals, remember that one type of food can contain more than one type of nutrient.

Sixty per cent of the human body is made up of water, so staying hydrated is vital if you want your body to function at its best. Hydration is particularly important for performers taking part in high-intensity or long-duration activities. The consequences of dehydration can be serious.

When you are **hydrated**, you have enough water in your body for it to function properly. You become **dehydrated** when your body does not contain enough water for it to function as efficiently as it should.

**Water helps to regulate body temperature through sweating and prevents you overheating:** It is important for your internal temperature to stay steady at 36.1–37.8°C, so your body has to get rid of the excess heat created by your muscles when you exercise, or you will overheat and can experience heatstroke or heat exhaustion. Vasodilation is one way the body gets rid of excess heat. Sweating is another. When the water in sweat evaporates it also takes some of your body heat with it. Dehydration reduces your body's ability to sweat and makes you more likely to overheat.

**Water keeps the joints lubricated:** Water is a key component of synovial fluid, a clear, slippery substance produced in joints to enable them to move smoothly through their full range of motion.

**Water keeps blood liquid thin so that it flows around the body easily:** Blood cells are carried in plasma, which is mainly water. When your blood does not contain a lot of plasma, it is thick and sticky; it is viscous. When you are dehydrated, your blood becomes viscous. Viscous blood does not flow well, which means that oxygen and other nutrients do not reach your working muscles as quickly as they do when your blood is less viscous – when you have more plasma and your blood is runnier.

**The benefits of hydration for sport and physical activity**

The recommended daily intake (RDI) of water is two litres per day, and this is sufficient under normal circumstances. However, you need to drink more fluids to maintain hydration when you are involved in sport and physical activity, to replace the water lost through sweat. Depending on the intensity and duration of the activity, as well as the weather conditions, you may need to increase your fluid intake quite considerably to avoid dehydration. Some sources recommend an additional one litre of fluid per hour while exercising in hot weather. The best way to judge if you need more liquid, though, is to listen to your body. Feeling thirsty is your body's way of telling you to drink more fluids. You can also look at the colour of your urine; if it is dark in colour and smells pungent you are almost certainly dehydrated.

You can get your water intake from a variety of sources, including fruit juice, milk, fizzy drinks, coffee, and tea, but drinking water is the best way to maintain hydration. Fruit and vegetables that are high in moisture, such as oranges and cucumbers, can also help keep you hydrated.

## B ronze

1. Using a 500ml water bottle to help you, keep a record of how much water you drink over the course of one week. At the same time, keep a record of the length of time you spend exercising and how hot the weather is. Use the data you collect to answer the following questions:

   a) What was your average daily intake on days you did not exercise and was it above the recommended daily intake (RDI)?

   b) Describe the effect your average daily intake of water will have had on your body. Were you generally hydrated or dehydrated and what did this mean for your body?

   c) What was your average daily intake on days you exercised?

   d) What effect did exercise have on your daily intake? Why?

Eating a healthy diet is not just about consuming all the macronutrients and micronutrients your body needs to function properly. It is also about consuming the right balance of nutrients and not consuming too much or too little. Sports performers can also manage their food intake to maximize their sporting performance and can consider taking legal supplements to boost their performance.

## Eating a healthy balanced diet

Like everyone else, sports performers should eat a healthy balanced diet to ensure they can train and compete successfully. A healthy balanced diet is a diet that contains the correct proportions of carbohydrates, protein, and fats, includes all the required micronutrients, and keeps you fully hydrated.

It is important to eat three meals a day and to ensure that each meal – breakfast, lunch, and dinner – contains the following proportions of macronutrients:

- carbohydrates, primarily complex carbohydrates and including fruit and vegetables: 50–60%
- fats, primarily unsaturated fats: 30%
- protein: 12–15%.

The 'Eatwell Guide' has been developed by the government to inform people of the proportions of different types of foods they should eat for a healthy balanced diet:

Excellent sources of carbohydrates and minerals. Wholegrain foods are also a good source of fibre.

Excellent sources of vitamins, minerals, and carbohydrates. Fruit and vegetables contain a lot of fibre.

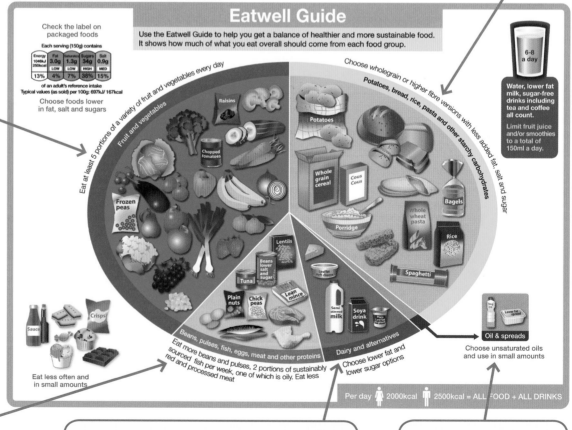

Excellent sources of protein, fats, vitamins, and minerals.

Excellent sources of fats, protein, and vitamins.

Excellent sources of fats.

## Improving your diet

The first step in improving a diet is working out how healthy or unhealthy it is to begin with. Is it missing or low in essential macronutrients or micronutrients, or is it too high in fats, particularly saturated fats, or simple carbohydrates? Once you have identified potential problems with the diet, you can begin to think about which foods should be consumed in greater quantities, and use this information to plan healthier meals.

For example, a student who eats a beef burger and chips for lunch each day is consuming far too much saturated fat and not enough fruit and vegetables. Although they will be getting iron and vitamin B1 from their beef, their diet is probably low in vitamin C and in the fibre that is essential for a healthy digestive system. To improve their diet, they should eat a range of different foods for lunch, opting for meals containing vegetables and choosing fruit as a snack.

## Eating the right amount of food

Eating a healthy diet involves making sure that the energy taken into the body through food and drink is matched by the amount of energy expended. If you take more energy than you expend into your body, you will put on weight. Energy is measured in **calories** (kcal).

The recommended daily allowance of calories for an adult male is 2500kcal. The recommended daily allowance of calories for an adult female is 2000kcal. However, the more exercise you do, the more energy you need and, consequently, the more calories you need to consume. The number of calories you need to consume is also affected by your age and your height; a younger person needs to consume more calories than an older person and a taller person needs to consume more calories than a shorter person.

→ *Most foods are labelled to show you how much of each macronutrient they contain and how many calories they contain.*

**1.** Five meals are described below. For each meal, draw a plate containing the meal, broken into its constituent food groups. Then compare the plate you have drawn with the 'Eatwell Guide'. Is the meal healthy or unhealthy?

   **a)** Pepperoni pizza, chips, and a fizzy orange drink.

   **b)** Spaghetti bolognaise and a glass of milk.

   **c)** Chicken salad followed by a blackberry tart, with a glass of water.

   **d)** Baked potato with cheese, beans, and salad, with a glass of fruit juice.

   **e)** Baked cod, baked potato, peas, and broccoli, with a glass of water.

### Silver

**2.** Next to each plate you drew for Activity 1, explain how you would make the meal healthier.

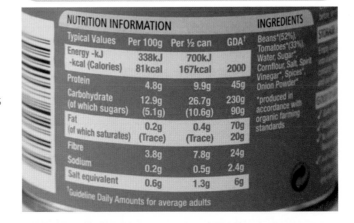

### Bronze

**3.** **a)** Keep a food diary of everything you eat and drink for three days, recording how many calories you consume.

   **b)** Search for 'Harris Benedict equation' in a search engine and use an online calculator to work out how many calories you need to consume each day to maintain a healthy weight. Remember to be honest about how active your lifestyle really is!

   **c)** Compare the number of calories you should be consuming each day with the number of calories you actually consume each day. Do you need to make a change to your diet?

   **d)** Explain what actions you will take to improve your diet.

# Eating to enhance sporting performance

Sports performers must not only eat a healthy balanced diet, they must also ensure that their diet is specifically tailored to their sport, their training programme, and their competition schedule.

## Before training and competition

When preparing for physical activity, performers must carefully consider what foods they eat and when they eat them. It is also important to drink plenty of fluids before taking part in sport and physical activity to avoid becoming dehydrated.

When preparing for intense aerobic exercise, performers must load their bodies with energy-providing foods containing carbohydrates to maximize their stores of glycogen. They will often eat complex carbohydrates in the days leading up to a competition and the night before a competition, a process that is referred to as '**carbohydrate loading**'. Immediately before a competition they may also eat something that is easy to digest and contains simple carbohydrates, such as toast and honey, to maximize the glucose available to them and to enable them to work at a high intensity right from the start.

It is easier to perform at your peak with an empty bowel, so many people recommend going to the toilet before exercise. Fibre is essential for healthy bowel function, so performers should eat a diet that is high in fibre to aid their digestion.

## During training and competition

Sports performers should ensure they drink plenty of fluids, in the form of water or a sports drink, if they are working at a high intensity, for a long period of time, or in hot weather, so that they remain hydrated. If the activity is lengthy, they may also require a snack. Foods that are easy to digest and contain simple carbohydrates for energy, such as a low-fat cereal bar or a banana, are best. Foods that contain protein may also be eaten, because they will help repair muscle damage.

## After training and competition

Sports drinks are popular with sports performers, particularly immediately after training and competition. Like water they help to rehydrate the body but they also contain electrolytes, to replace the electrolytes lost through sweat, and simple carbohydrates, to give the body a boost of energy.

Within one or two hours of training or competing, it is sensible to eat a meal containing complex carbohydrates, to replenish the body's store of glycogen, and protein, to help repair muscle damage and promote muscle growth. Strength and power performers, such as weightlifters, may also consume additional protein in the form of protein shakes to help them to achieve hypertrophy.

**B** **ronze**

4. Create a three-day meal plan for a sports performer of your choice. The plan should cover the day before a competition, the day of the competition, and the day after the competition. It should include breakfast, lunch, and dinner, as well as drinks and snacks.

In 2016, Glenn Kearney, the nutritionist for the GB Davis Cup team, spoke to *Men's Health* magazine about the food Andy Murray and the other members of the team ate during the competition. Here's what he said:

### First serve

*For breakfast, players like Andy Murray have freshly squeezed juice and either a medium bowl of muesli with berries and yoghurt or porridge with toppings. This is always followed up with a plate of eggs, bacon, and baked beans. You can't beat tradition for fuelling a heavy training session.*

### Middle set

*After a morning training session, lunch is a DIY fruit smoothie, followed by a full cooked meal with fairly even proportions of lean protein, nutritious vegetables, and some carbohydrates. If the session was particularly brutal then I make sure the players will increase their carb proportions to refuel.*

### Match point

*When it comes to dinner, the pros start off with soup, seafood, or salad starters. This is followed by a main course that usually consists of a chicken, potato, and vegetables combo. If the afternoon training is particularly draining then side dishes of spinach, green beans, brown rice, and pasta will increase to speed up recovery.*

Source: www.menshealth.co.uk/food-nutrition/how-to-eat-like-andy-murray

# Taking supplements to enhance sporting performance

Although most of us can get all the nutrients we require from the food we eat, some sports performers take supplements to enhance their performance or to aid recovery. Here are a selection of supplements and the ways in which they enhance performance:

→ *The B vitamins are a group of vitamins that occur together in foods. Vitamin B1 breaks down the carbohydrates we eat into energy, so a lack of vitamin B1 in your diet may result in a reduction in performance. Supplementing vitamin B1 can benefit some endurance athletes as a result.*

→ *Vitamin D is crucial for healthy bones, so increasing the vitamin D in your diet by taking vitamin D tablets will make your bones stronger and healthier. This is beneficial for all sports performers but particularly those who take part in high-impact activities or contact sports.*

→ *Protein supplements usually come as a powder that you mix with water or milk to form a protein shake, and are often drunk after a strength or power training session. Most provide all eight essential amino acids. Protein is essential for muscle growth and repair, so can help a performer train harder for longer and with less recovery time.*

→ *Pre-workout supplements are designed to give you a boost of energy before exercise. There are many different types of pre-workout supplement, and it is important to choose one that supports the type of exercise you are about to do; someone taking part in an aerobic endurance training session will take a very different pre-workout supplement from someone taking part in a strength or power training session.*

→ *Isotonic drinks containing glucose replenish electrolytes lost through sweat and help a performer rehydrate. They also provide a burst of energy to enable performers to work at a greater intensity or to recover from intense exercise.*

→ *Caffeine can improve alertness and concentration, and studies have shown it can improve aerobic endurance and power.*

**B ronze**

5. Research the side effects of the six supplements described above and prepare a poster warning people of the disadvantages of consuming too much of each supplement.

It is very important to understand that you can have too much of a good thing, and all food and drink supplements have side effects if you consume too much.

Simon is a 26-year-old man and he has been keeping a food diary. Here is an extract from that food diary, showing everything he ate and drank in one day:

| Day | Time | Food and drink consumed | Calories consumed |
|---|---|---|---|
| Wednesday | 7.30 a.m. | **Grapefruit**: 16.4g carbohydrates (of which 16.4g sugar), 3.2g fibre, < 1g fat (of which < 0.2g saturated fat), 0g protein | 82kcal |
| | | **400ml water**: 0g carbohydrates, 0g fibre, 0g fat, 0g protein | 0kcal |
| | 10.00 a.m. | **Cereal bar**: 27.1g carbohydrates (of which 11.9g sugar), 2.4g fibre, 7.2g fat (of which 1g saturated fat), 3.4g protein | 192kcal |
| | | **250ml cup of tea with semi-skimmed milk**: 2g carbohydrates (of which 2g sugar), 0g fibre, 1g fat (of which 1g saturated fat), 1g protein | 23kcal |
| | 1.00 p.m. | **Chicken and bacon sandwich**: 73.6g carbohydrates (of which 7.3g sugar), 2.6g fibre, 29.9g fat (of which 4.7g saturated fat), 31.3g protein | 693kcal |
| | | **Packet of crisps**: 13.3g carbohydrates (of which 0.5g sugar), 1.1g fibre, 7.6g fat (of which 0.6g saturated fat), 1.5g protein | 130kcal |
| | | **330ml diet cola**: 0g carbohydrates, 0g fibre, 0g fat, 0g protein | 1kcal |
| | 4.00 p.m. | **Banana**: 26.9g carbohydrates (of which 24.3g sugar), 1.3g fibre, < 0.6g fat (of which < 0.1g saturated fat), 1.4g protein | 119kcal |
| | | **400ml water**: 0g carbohydrates, 0g fibre, 0g fat, 0g protein | 0kcal |
| | 7.00 p.m. | **Vegetarian chilli and white rice** (the chilli contains sweet potatoes, bell peppers, onion, garlic, kidney beans, tinned tomatoes, chillies, olive oil, and spices): 123g carbohydrates (of which 29g sugar), 30g fibre, 17.5g fat (of which 3g saturated fat), 32g protein | 835kcal |
| | | **200ml orange juice**: 17.8g carbohydrates (of which 17.8g sugar), 1.2g fibre, 0g fat, 1.6g protein | 86kcal |
| | 10.00 p.m. | **400ml water**: 0g carbohydrates, 0g fibre, 0g fat, 0g protein | 0kcal |

## Bronze

6. Look at Simon's food diary. Is he eating a healthy balanced diet? Explain your answer, using examples from the food diary.

## Silver

7. How could Simon improve his diet? Make three recommendations, giving reasons for each recommendation.

## Gold

8. Imagine that Simon is training for a marathon. How should he alter his diet to maximize his chances of finishing the marathon in a good time?

There is a psychological aspect to sporting success. Successful sports performers train hard, but they are also mentally strong. They are motivated to succeed and it is this motivation that provides them with the focus and drive to do well. But motivation is not just important for famous sports performers; it also plays an important role in helping us all stick to our sport and exercise goals.

## What is motivation?

The internal mechanisms are described as **intrinsic motivation**. These are sources of motivation that come from within a person. Examples of intrinsic motivation include taking part in sport and physical exercise because you enjoy being part of a team, because you want to gain experience of competing at a certain level, or because you get a sense of self-worth from your achievements.

**Motivation** is a combination of the internal mechanisms and external stimuli that arouse and direct behaviour.

The external stimuli are described as **extrinsic motivation**. These are sources of motivation that come from outside a person, and they can be tangible or intangible. Examples of tangible extrinsic motivation include rewards such as trophies, money, and records: things you can touch. Examples of intangible extrinsic motivation include praise and encouragement, as well as fear of loss of status: things you cannot touch.

> *I hated every minute of training but I said, 'Don't quit. Suffer now and live the rest of your life as a champion.'*
> **Muhammad Ali**

### B ronze

1. Read the quote from Muhammad Ali. Does it demonstrate intrinsic or extrinsic motivation?

# The benefits of increased motivation

### Intensity of effort is higher
A sports performer who possesses high levels of intrinsic and/or extrinsic motivation will channel all their effort into ensuring they perform to the best of their ability in order to succeed. As the performer's desire to succeed becomes more intense, so too will the level of effort they put into their training and competitions.

### Participation is regular
A sports performer who possesses high levels of intrinsic and/or extrinsic motivation will keep at it. They will return to the gym, to the pool, or to the pitch week after week, come rain or shine, because they know that regular participation is the best way to meet their goals.

### Persistence in adversity is greater
A motivated sports performer is much more likely to overcome adversity than a performer who lacks motivation. This is because a performer who possesses high levels of intrinsic and/or extrinsic motivation will find it easier to keep going when things get difficult. For example, they will have the strength of will to battle back from serious injury.

**The benefits of motivation for participation**

### Enjoyment is higher
A motivated sports performer will enjoy what they are doing much more than a performer who lacks motivation. This is not to say that they will enjoy every training session or every competition, but someone who is motivated will be able to look beyond current setbacks or immediate discomfort and say that they enjoy what they are doing.

### Intrinsic and extrinsic rewards are greater
A sports performer who experiences intrinsic and/or extrinsic rewards from participation will feel more motivated the more they participate, because the more they participate the more rewards they will receive.

## S ilver

2. Read Joe's story and explain how motivation will have helped him become an athlete after his life-changing injuries. Remember to discuss intrinsic sources of motivation and extrinsic sources of motivation.

> Joe Townsend is a former Royal Marine Commando who lost both legs in an explosion while serving in Afghanistan in 2008, aged 19. Following a lengthy rehabilitation programme, Joe decided he wanted to return to the fitness levels he had enjoyed as a Royal Marine by competing in his first Ironman UK triathlon competition. In 2018, he won a Commonwealth gold medal in the Paratriathlon.

# The impact self-confidence can have on participation in sport and activity

Taking up a new sport or physical activity, or continuing to participate when things are challenging, requires positive thinking. You need to believe in yourself, and to believe that you can succeed. In other words, you need to have self-confidence. Sports leaders play an important role in helping people increase their self-confidence.

## What is self-confidence?

**Self-confidence** is the belief that a desired behaviour can be performed. It is believing in who you are, in your abilities, and in your judgement. It is believing that you can perform a cartwheel, that you can score a goal, or that you can run a marathon.

> " *It is not the mountain we conquer, but ourselves.*
> **Sir Edmund Hillary** "

### B ronze

1.  Read the quote from Sir Edmund Hillary. Tenzing Norgay and Sir Edmund Hillary were the first people to reach the summit of Mount Everest. How do you think self-confidence helped them do this?

## The benefits of self-confidence

**Performance is improved**
A sports performer with self-confidence is going to perform better than a sports performer without self-confidence. For example, a performer who takes the criticisms of their peers or coach to heart and lets them sow seeds of doubt about their ability will not perform as well as a performer who listens to the criticisms and uses them to fuel their personal development while continuing to believe in their own abilities.

**The benefits of self-confidence for participation**

**Intrinsic motivation increases**
Self-confidence is closely linked to intrinsic motivation. If you believe in yourself and your abilities you are more likely to be motivated by factors within yourself. Winning trophies may still be important to you, but the feelings generated by taking part and doing your best are more likely to drive you onwards and help you increase your participation.

**Concentration and effort will be improved**
A sports performer is more likely to remain focused on the task at hand if they believe that they have the ability to succeed. A performer with low self-confidence may lose concentration and become distracted by people around them, by other competitors, the crowd, or their coach. If a performer has low self-confidence they are also more likely to crumble under pressure and give up at the first hurdle.

**Positive attitude is increased**
Someone with self-confidence is more likely to have a positive attitude towards sport and physical activity. They believe they can succeed at anything they set their mind to, and so approach sport and physical activity confident that they can reach their goals if they put in the time and effort.

# Methods to increase self-confidence

There is a range of different methods that sports leaders can use to help participants increase their self-confidence.

**Providing intrinsic motivation through positive reinforcement**
Positive reinforcement is about encouraging a particular behaviour or attitude by offering a reward when that behaviour or attitude is exhibited. Sports leaders can use positive reinforcement to increase self-confidence, by offering praise and encouragement when a performer does something they thought they could not do. This praise and encouragement is a form of extrinsic motivation.

**Creating a positive environment**
Sports leaders play a very important role in creating a positive environment for participants. If they are friendly, welcoming, enthusiastic, and knowledgeable, if they actively listen and communicate clearly, then participants are going to be more relaxed and feel more comfortable exercising. The participants will perform better as a result and this will boost their self-confidence.

**Encouraging participants to choose a training partner of a similar ability**
Working with a training partner who is at a similar level to you can increase your self-confidence. When you look at your partner's achievements, you will see your own achievements reflected back at you. Sometimes you will be better than they are and sometimes they will be better than you, and the competition between you will encourage you both to work harder. A sports leader can encourage participants to choose the right partner.

**Helping participants to set realistic goals**
Sports leaders can help participants set realistic goals, for an individual training session or for a whole training programme. Participants are much more likely to achieve realistic goals, boosting their self-confidence. Aiming for unrealistic goals can be very demoralizing and really knock a participant's self-confidence.

**Teaching participants the technique of positive self-talk**
Positive self-talk is a technique that involves a participant running an internal commentary that encourages self-confidence and turns any negative thoughts into positive thoughts. For example, they might tell themselves that diving from the diving board for the first time is a great adventure and nothing to be scared of, that they can do it, and that they will enjoy it.

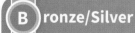 **B** **ronze/Silver**

2. **a)** Think of a situation in which you didn't feel confident about your sporting performance and jot down what happened.
   **b)** Write a paragraph about the impact of self-confidence on sporting performance, using your own experience as an example.
   **c)** Explain how a sports leader could have improved your self-confidence in the situation you have been thinking about.

 **Link**

You can find out how to help participants set realistic goals using the SMART target-setting technique on page 109.

Anxiety about taking part in sport and physical activity can put people off participating in the first place. Anxiety about how well they are going to perform can make people turn away from sport and physical activity even if they once enjoyed it. And anxiety can stop people performing at their best. There are, however, many ways to manage anxiety, so that people can experience the physical and psychological benefits of getting active.

## What is anxiety?

**Anxiety** is the level of nervousness or worry that a participant experiences.

There are two types of anxiety:

1. **State anxiety**
   **State anxiety** is temporary. It is brought on by specific high-pressure situations that make a person feel anxious and activate their nervous system. For example, a competitive swimmer may experience high levels of state anxiety before they are called to their starting position, anxiety that usually settles as they begin the race.

2. **Trait anxiety**
   A 'trait' is a personality characteristic. **Trait anxiety** is a fixed or relatively permanent form of anxiety, which people suffer from because their nervous system is constantly active. A person with trait anxiety is generally considered to have an anxiety disorder and will display signs of anxiousness regularly in different, often non-threatening situations. Trait anxiety is innate, which means you are born with it.

State anxiety and trait anxiety can display themselves in two different ways. From the outside the effects look very similar but they feel very different on the inside:

**Somatic anxiety**
**Somatic anxiety** has a physical effect on the body and can make a performer feel ill. Symptoms of somatic anxiety include feeling butterflies in your stomach, muscle tension, an increase in your heart rate, and an increase in the amount you sweat.

**Cognitive anxiety**
**Cognitive anxiety** has a psychological effect on the mind. It can make a performer worry more than is necessary, it can lower a performer's ability to concentrate, and it can cause a performer to suffer from insomnia when they cannot get to sleep because thoughts are whirling around their head.

### Bronze

1. Think of a situation in which you have experienced state anxiety. Describe how you felt and decide whether you think you were experiencing somatic anxiety or cognitive anxiety.

# Methods to control anxiety

There is a range of different methods that sports leaders can use to help participants manage their anxiety, particularly their state anxiety.

**Familiarizing participants with the facilities**
Taking the time to show participants around the facilities so that they know where to go and how the equipment works can help to reduce their anxiety. This is especially important when participants will be training on their own, as they often are in a gym, and, along with health and safety considerations, is one of the reasons why gym inductions are so important.

**Playing music that lowers anxiety and increases motivation**
Music can play with our emotions. It can make us feel happy or sad, it can pump us up and motivate us, or it can calm us down and reduce our anxiety. Allowing participants to choose music that matches their mood can, therefore, have a very positive effect on participation. It is important to remember that different types of music have different effects on different people, so it may be necessary to encourage participants to listen to music through headphones.

**Encouraging participants to take part in activity sessions that suit their ability**
Finding yourself in an advanced dance class when you have no formal dance training, for example, can be incredibly stressful. A very simple way of reducing a participant's anxiety is, therefore, to make sure they are joining a class, a club, or a league that suits their ability. Then they can relax and enjoy developing their skills alongside other participants at the same level.

**Introducing a pre-match team talk**
A pre-match team talk, from a coach or the team captain, can reassure players, reducing their anxiety and increasing their motivation. Clearly setting out the team's strategy for the game, acknowledging and minimizing challenges, and emphasizing the team's strengths can help players focus on the game ahead and limit the negative thoughts that can lead to anxiety.

 **G**old

2. **a)** Rate your feelings of anxiety on a scale of 1–5, choosing 1 if you are not feeling anxious at all and 5 if you are feeling very anxious.
   **b)** Listen to five very different pieces of music for three minutes each and, after each piece of music, rate your feelings of anxiety, again on a scale of 1–5.
   **c)** Analyse your response to the different pieces of music. Which made you feel more anxious and which made you feel calmer?
   **d)** Evaluate how effective music is for managing anxiety.

Component 2 will be assessed by a written exam lasting one and a half hours. You will be expected to answer all the questions on the exam paper in this time.

## Assessment objectives

When you answer the questions on the exam paper you will be expected to do three things:

**AO1** → Demonstrate knowledge of the principles of training to improve fitness, nutrition, and psychological influences.

**AO2** → Demonstrate understanding of training to improve fitness, nutrition, and psychological influences when applying to sport and activity.

**AO3** → Analyse and evaluate data and information in relation to fitness, nutrition, and psychological influences when applying to sport and activity.

## Tackling the assessment

The first thing you need to do when you open the exam paper is take a deep breath and let it out slowly. This will help reduce any anxiety you have carried into the exam room with you. Remind yourself that you can do this!

One of the most common mistakes learners make is not answering the question they have been asked, so you need to decode each exam question before you start writing your answer. This is a three-step process:

1. Underline the command word, the word that is telling you what to do. Common command words include:
   - **State**, which is asking you to give a definition or an example. The question will usually require one definition or example per mark.
   - **Name**, which is asking you to identify something by name. The question will usually require one name per mark.

- **Give**, which is asking you to provide exactly what is requested. It could be a reason, an example, a definition, and so on. The question will usually require one reason, example, or definition per mark.
- **Identify**, which is asking you to indicate who or what something is. The question will usually require one thing to be identified per mark.
- **Calculate**, which is asking you to perform a mathematical calculation to determine a numerical value. The question will usually require one numerical value per mark.
- **Explain**, which is asking you to show that you understand something by making a point and then developing that point with an additional piece of information, an example, or a statement of your opinion. Explain questions are usually worth two marks: one mark for the initial point and one mark for the development.
- **Describe**, which is asking you to give a clear account of something. Look at the number of marks allocated to describe questions to work out how much you are expected to write. Aim to write one sentence for each mark.
- **Discuss**, which is asking you to consider different aspects of the topic and how they relate to each other. Discuss questions are usually worth nine marks, and to score high marks you must demonstrate that your knowledge is accurate, the points you make are relevant to the question, and that your discussion is logical and detailed.
- **Evaluate**, which is asking you to look at the advantages and disadvantages, strengths and weaknesses, or pros and cons of something, and then come to a justified judgement on which perspective is strongest. Evaluate questions are usually worth nine marks and to score high marks you must demonstrate that your knowledge is accurate, that the points you make are relevant to the question, that your evaluation is logical, and that you come to a reasoned conclusion.
- **Analyse**, which is asking you to examine each part of something methodically in order to demonstrate something. Analyse questions are usually worth nine marks and to score high marks you must ensure your analysis is sufficiently detailed and that each sentence you write relates directly to the something at the heart of the question.

2. Circle any words in bold in the question. If you are asked to 'give **two** reasons', you must give two reasons to score full marks. If you make two points about one reason you will only score half marks.

3. Identify the topic and sub-topic the question is about. Is it about fitness training? Nutrition? Motivation? Self-confidence? Anxiety? And if it is about nutrition, is it about macronutrients, micronutrients, hydration, or about nutrition for specific sports performers?

Revising thoroughly before the exam and following these three simple steps will put you in a strong position to do well in your exam.

## Example answers to questions from the Sample Assessment Materials for this qualification

Natalie's netball team has been training hard and she has made it to the national finals. She is anxious about the game.

(a) Give the definition of anxiety. (1)

Being nervous or scared about the outcome of situations.

1 mark. This is a good definition of anxiety.

(b) Explain how state anxiety can affect Natalie's participation in sport and physical activity. (2)

State anxiety is a temporary form of anxiety that involves the activation of the nervous system in high-pressure situations. It could have been brought on because of the pressure of the final and it may cause Natalie to be nervous before the event.

2 marks. 1 mark for defining state anxiety and 1 mark for describing Natalie's physical response to state anxiety.

(c) Explain **two** methods that Natalie's coach could use to control players' anxiety levels.

1. When the players are getting ready in the changing rooms before the final, the coach could play music to the players. The coach should choose music that relaxes all the players or encourage players to listen to their own choice of music through headphones. (2)

2 marks. 1 mark for identifying that playing music is a suitable method for controlling anxiety and 1 mark for providing more detail about that method and how it will help the players control their anxiety.

2. The coach should also remind the players of the importance of the game. (2)

0 marks. This is not a suitable method for helping the players control their anxiety and there is no expansion as to why the method may help.

**(Total for Question = 7 marks)**

Chaneece needs to improve her speed on the football pitch.

Evaluate which one of these training methods Chaneece should use to improve her speed when playing football.

- Sprint training.
- Speed, Agility and Quickness (SAQ). (9)

Sprint training is an effective way to improve speed in football because it involves short sprints that are similar to the sprints required during a match when chasing a through-ball or chasing an opponent to make a tackle. Chaneece could mark out short sprint distances on a football pitch, developing her speed in a similar environment to the conditions of a match. A disadvantage to sprint training is that it only trains straight-line running speed. As previously mentioned this is a useful thing to train, but it does not involve changes of direction, which are sometimes required in football.

SAQ training focuses on speed, agility, and quickness. Ladders, hurdles, and vertical poles are used to replicate a range of different twists and turns that take place in football. In this way, SAQ training trains multiple movement patterns and changes of direction, not just straight-line speed. SAQ equipment does cost money though, so whether or not it would be appropriate for Chaneece will depend on how much money her club has.

Both sprint and SAQ training would bring about improvements in speed for football. Chaneece will also see improvements in strength and muscular endurance as she will constantly be contracting her muscles over time, making them bigger and stronger. Considering the pros and cons of both methods, Chaneece could use a combination of the two to ensure her training sessions are varied and she does not get bored. Getting the benefits of both training methods will enable Chaneece to improve her straight-line speed and her agility and quickness.

This is a Level 3 answer, which will score 7–9 marks. It has a strong structure. The first paragraph looks at the advantages and disadvantages of sprint training, the second paragraph looks at the advantages and disadvantages of SAQ training, and the third paragraph draws a conclusion. Throughout, the answer makes strong links between the methods of training being discussed and Chaneece and the demands of football.

## Exam practice

1  Rosie is a gymnast and, to progress, she realizes she needs to work on improving her flexibility and her strength.

   (a) Give the definition of flexibility. (1)

   (b) State **two** methods of training designed to improve flexibility. (2)

   (c) Explain **one** advantage of training with free weights for Rosie. (2)

   (d) Explain **one** disadvantage of training with free weights for Rosie. (2)

**(Total for Question 1 = 7 marks)**

2  Steven is a sprint cyclist. His weekly training programme looks like this:

| Monday | Continuous training in the swimming pool |
|---|---|
| Wednesday | Core stability training |
| Saturday | Sport-specific speed training on his bike |

Discuss how effectively Steven is applying the principle of specificity to his training programme. (9)

**(Total for Question 2 = 9 marks)**

3  Jahan is managing a football team at his local leisure centre. He notices that a number of the players are lacking self-confidence.

   (a) Give the definition of self-confidence. (1)

   (b) Name **two** methods Jahan could use to increase the self-confidence of the team. (2)

   (c) Increased self-confidence leads to an increase in intrinsic motivation. Explain what intrinsic motivation is. (2)

   (d) Explain **two** benefits of high levels of intrinsic motivation for participation. (4)

**(Total for Question 3 = 9 marks)**

4  Lily wants to run a marathon and she has been told that eating the right foods is an important part of preparing for the event.

Discuss what Lily should eat while she is training, the night before the marathon, and immediately before the marathon. (9)

**(Total for Question 4 = 9 marks)**

5  Eddie plays basketball and he feels very thirsty when he plays a full match. His coach recommends he takes a look at his hydration.

   (a) What is the recommended daily intake (RDI) of water on a day with no exercise? (1)

   (b) Give the definition of dehydration. (1)

   (c) Identify **two** situations in which Eddie should drink more than the RDI of water. (2)

   (d) Explain **one** benefit of hydration to Eddie. (2)

   (e) Explain **one** disadvantage of dehydration to Eddie. (2)

**(Total for Question 5 = 8 marks)**

6  Rowan competes in the 400m hurdles. She has always been an anxious person, but her anxiety is increasing dramatically in the 24 hours before a race.

Evaluate the extent to which Rowan's anxiety is holding her back from performing at her best and the extent to which her coach will be able to help her control her anxiety in the run-up to a race. (9)

**(Total for Question 6 = 9 marks)**

# 3

# Applying the principles of sport and activity

Raheem is starting his first job as a Coaching Assistant for the Sports Development team at his local council. He has completed his BTEC Tech Award in Sport, Activity and Fitness and he will be using the knowledge he gained and the skills he developed during the course to help coach after-school sports clubs at a local leisure centre. This experience will also support Raheem as he begins his level 3 sports qualification at a local college.

This chapter will explore:

## Learning aim A: Understand the fundamentals of sport and activity leadership

→ 3.A1 The attributes of a leader

→ 3.A2 The benefits of participation in sport and activity sessions

## Learning aim B: Planning sessions for target groups

→ 3.B1 Target groups

→ 3.B2 Types of sessions

→ 3.B3 Session plan

## Learning aim C: Delivering and reviewing sessions for target groups

→ 3.C1 Methods of delivery/success

→ 3.C2 Methods of reviewing

You will have taken part in sport and activity sessions and experienced the skills and qualities that sports leaders – coaches, team managers, PE teachers – possess. Think about how the leaders you have worked with have interacted with you and the groups you have been part of. What were they good at and how can you develop the same skills and qualities?

## The skills of a sports leader

### Communication

Leaders need to be able to communicate instructions and feedback to participants to get the best out of the group they are leading. There are two types of communication:

### 1. Verbal communication

Verbal communication is using words to express yourself.

It is essential to think about your audience before you communicate verbally, ensuring the vocabulary you use is appropriate for your audience. For example, young children who have only just begun to take part in sport will lack the technical vocabulary that you may be able to use with older, more advanced participants.

When communicating verbally, it is as important to think about how you say the words as it is to choose the words you use carefully. For example, you can vary the tone and volume of your voice to convey different messages. Speaking with a harsh tone of voice very, very loudly gives an audience a very different message than speaking with a warm tone of voice loudly, even if the words are exactly the same.

### 2. Non-verbal communication

Non-verbal communication is the use of body language, gestures, and eye contact to convey your message.

It includes the use of hand signals to communicate with a group across a large area, and using your body to give clear demonstrations of techniques and drills. Thinking carefully about the message your body language is sending out is also an important part of non-verbal communication. If you arrive to play sport or take part in an activity session and your coach has their back to you and is checking their mobile phone, you may feel unwelcome and discouraged. In contrast, if your coach is facing you, smiling, and making eye contact with you when you arrive, then you are more likely to feel positive, engaged, and ready to work hard.

It can also be valuable to adapt your non-verbal communication to meet the needs of different participants. For example, when coaching small children it is helpful if your facial expression mirrors what you are saying. Asking the children if they are happy, and supporting this question with a happy face and a thumbs up, helps the children better understand what is being asked of them.

1. Repeat the following sentence, emphasizing a different word each time: 'I didn't say you stole my purse.' How does the word you emphasize change the meaning of what you are saying?

2. Look at these photographs of people communicating non-verbally. What message is each person conveying?

a)

b)

c)

d)

e)

## Listening

It is easy to forget to listen. Sometimes sports leaders are so busy running sessions and giving commands that they forget to take the time to listen to participants' concerns or feedback or – worse – they assume they know it all and participants should just get on and do as they are told. If you have ever tried to communicate with someone you feel is not listening to you, then you know how frustrating it can be. Participants who do not feel they are being listened to can quickly lose interest in the session.

To improve your listening skills, try the following active listening techniques:

- Show that you are interested and trying to understand what is being said to you by giving your full attention to the person who is talking. Maintain good eye contact and think about your body language. For example, face the person who is talking to you, nod to show you are thinking about what they are saying, and avoid standing with your arms crossed, which can make you look disinterested or defensive.
- Check that you have understood what has been said to you by summarizing the concern that has been raised and what the person has said they need from you.
- Respect what the person has to say and respond in an appropriate manner. Make it clear that you understand their concerns and their needs, and explain what you can do to help. If you cannot help directly, can you direct them to someone who can help or can you explain what is preventing you from helping?

Finally, remember to observe participants' non-verbal communication as well as their verbal communication. They might not come and tell you that they are bored, but can you observe, from their body language, that they want to move on?

3. Consider the following active listening techniques and describe how each technique helps the speaker feel that you are really listening to them:

a) eye contact

b) nodding

c) summarizing what the speaker has said to you

d) responding appropriately to what the speaker has said.

## Organization and activity structure

A well-organized session sets the right tone for participants. A session that starts on time, with all the equipment and playing surfaces already checked and ready to use, sends a clear non-verbal signal that the leader expects participants to engage, focus, and work hard. Similarly, a session that ends on time, with all the equipment properly packed away in the right places, shows that the leader respects their colleagues and recognizes that they are part of a wider coaching team.

A good plan is the secret to being organized. It helps a leader think through everything they need to do before, during, and after a session well before the session starts. It also provides a structure for a session, which the leader can follow. A good plan will provide participants with the opportunity to make progress during the session and will motivate participants to improve their physical health and their sporting skills and techniques.

## Knowledge

A successful sports leader is knowledgeable, and uses that knowledge to deliver a well-structured session and to coach participants. They will know how to lead a warm-up that prepares participants for the main component that follows, and they will know how to lead a cool-down that ensures participants' body systems gradually recover after exercise. They will be able to demonstrate relevant skills and techniques and provide guidance on how participants can develop. They will also be able to advise participants on the latest technology and how it can help them improve their performance.

### B ronze

5. **a)** Think of a sports leader who demonstrates knowledge of the sport they coach. How do you know they have this knowledge and how do you use it to run effective sessions?

   **b)** What technology does the sports leader you are thinking of use to help participants improve their performance?

### B ronze

4. Sam is a sports leader running a football session. Read Sam's story and describe how the participants in the session might have felt as a result of Sam's poor organizational skills.

> Sam turns up late because the traffic was heavy, as it is every afternoon. As a result, he hasn't had a chance to check all the equipment before the session begins and it turns out he doesn't have enough bibs to separate the group into two teams. As the session progresses, it becomes clear that Sam has forgotten to bring his session plan with him. The session has no clear aims and objectives and is very disjointed.

## Evaluating progress and setting targets for improvement

Most people who take part in sport and activity sessions want to progress. They want to get fitter or they want to get better at playing a particular sport. A successful sports leader will understand what each participant wants to achieve and will regularly evaluate their performance and their engagement to work out what they need to do to continue to develop. They will then set them targets to help them reach their goals.

It is also important to evaluate your own development as a sports leader and set yourself targets for improvement. You can find out more about how to do this on pages 152–154.

### Set SMART targets

> I want you to work hard and get better at this drill by the end of the session.

> I want you to give more effort and get it right.

You hear statements like these all the time in sport and activity sessions, but they are very general and not terribly helpful. To set targets that motivate participants, you must set SMART targets:

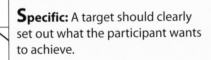

**Specific:** A target should clearly set out what the participant wants to achieve.

**Measurable:** There should be a way of working out if the participant has achieved a target.

**Achievable:** A target should be appropriate to the fitness and skill level of the participant.

**Realistic:** A target should be possible given the ability of the participant and their role within the activity.

**Time-bound:** A point by which the target should have been achieved should be specified.

**B** ronze

6. Three participants have shared their SMART targets with you. For each person:
   a) identify the problem with their SMART target
   b) describe the effect the SMART target will have on the participant
   c) rewrite the SMART target so that it is more motivating.

> I am going to score 12 goals in the next 10 matches by 1st January.
>
> *12-year-old footballer, who plays as a defender for their local team.*

> I am going to get 100% of my first serves in over the next three tennis matches.
>
> *25-year-old tennis player, who plays in a county league.*

> I am going to improve my goalkeeping skills by Christmas.
>
> *15-year-old hockey goalkeeper, who plays recreationally with a group of friends.*

## The qualities of a sports leader

### Motivating

A sports leader can have a wealth of knowledge and be very skilled at the sport they are coaching but, without the ability to motivate participants, they may not lead successful sessions.

Here are six techniques for motivating participants:

- **Be enthusiastic!** This is most important, because enthusiasm is infectious.
- **Have fun:** It is possible for participants to work hard and make progress while having fun, so make sure that sessions are enjoyable. This will increase participants' intrinsic motivation.
- **Give praise:** Focus on the process as well as the outcome, praising a participant who has listened to instructions and worked hard to improve as well as a participant who has performed successfully. Praise provides extrinsic motivation.
- **Give rewards:** Rewards work particularly well with younger participants. You could award a prize for best performance or best effort, or award a certificate for attendance or learning new skills. Rewards provide extrinsic motivation.
- **Set targets:** Set meaningful targets for each session and work with participants to set personal targets that will help them achieve their long-term goals. Targets, particularly SMART targets, provide extrinsic motivation.
- **Give feedback:** Providing regular feedback helps participants feel involved. It feels good to know someone is taking note of your hard work and wants to help you get better. Feedback provides extrinsic motivation.

### Inspires confidence

The government expects the sport and fitness industry to encourage more people to take part in sport and physical activity so that they can experience the many physical and psychological benefits of an active lifestyle. A sports leader needs to inspire confidence in people who may never have joined a fitness class or tried a particular sport before, helping them overcome any fears they might have. A sports leader that encourages participants and regularly recognizes how far they have come will help to build participants' self-confidence, which will, in turn, motivate them to maintain a physically active lifestyle.

 **Link**

Remind yourself of the difference between intrinsic motivation and extrinsic motivation on page 94.

 **B** ronze

7. Research a person you consider to be successful from outside the world of sport. Prepare a short presentation about what motivates your chosen person and describe how you could make use of the motivational techniques they employ during an activity session. Remember to consider intrinsic and extrinsic motivation.

 **Link**

Remind yourself of the benefits of self-confidence and the methods a sports leader can use to increase participants' self-confidence on pages 96–97.

 **B** ronze

8. Read Isaac's story and describe how the five-a-side football coach can inspire confidence in Isaac, so that he keeps attending the training sessions.

> Isaac is a middle-aged man who struggles to maintain a healthy weight. He has tried many different diets and joined gyms numerous times but always stops going after a few weeks because he never feels like he is making any progress. Recently, Isaac has joined a local five-a-side football team in an attempt to lose some weight.

## Personality

Your personality is a collection of characteristics that make you who you are. Everyone's personality is unique but psychologists have developed two different ways of characterizing people based on their personality.

### Introverts and extroverts

**Introverts** are shy people who are generally happy in their own company. **Extroverts** are confident and outgoing. They enjoy socializing and are generally very comfortable in other people's company.

### Type A personalities and Type B personalities

**Type A** people are:

- impatient
- time-conscious
- competitive
- outgoing
- aggressive
- driven
- forceful
- focused
- rushed.

**Type B** people are:

- patient
- relaxed
- lazy
- tolerant
- easy-going
- calm
- passive
- stress-free
- laid-back.

People who do not fit into either category are classed as type AB.

Whether you are an introvert or an extrovert may affect the type of sports you take part in. For example, an extrovert may be more likely to enjoy taking part in team sports, such as football or hockey, whereas an introvert may prefer individual sports in which they can work alone, such as cycling or swimming.

While there is no evidence to suggest that success as a leader is dependent on the type of personality you have, your personality may affect your approach to sports leadership. For example:

→ *Jürgen Klopp is extremely competitive and outgoing. He regularly displays his Type A personality on the touchline, encouraging his players to work harder in tough situations.*

→ *Gareth Southgate is not very animated on the touchline, but his Type B personality conveys trust in his players who respond positively to his calm, patient approach.*

### B ronze

9.  **a)** Are you an introvert or an extrovert? Write a paragraph describing your personality and decide whether you are an introvert or an extrovert.

    **b)** Are you a Type A or a Type B personality? List eight characteristics that you have and decide whether you are Type A, Type B, or Type AB.

    **c)** Explain how your personality will make you a successful sports leader.

## Leadership styles

Sports leaders use a variety of leadership styles, depending on what they want to achieve and the types of participants they are working with. There are three leadership styles:

### Autocratic

An **autocratic leader** has absolute power, making all the decisions and imposing these decisions on their group.

An autocratic leadership style is helpful when dealing with very young children who need to be given clear instructions and clear boundaries. This is because young children like to 'follow the leader' and, often, will not question the task they are asked to do.

Using an autocratic leadership style is also sensible if you are leading larger group activities that involve potential hazards or have an element of danger, such as supervising javelin throwing practice or leading a high-ropes course. This is because the leader needs to be in control to keep participants safe; participants doing things their own way could lead to very serious injuries.

**B**ronze

**10.** Which famous sports leaders are known for having an autocratic leadership style and what effect does their leadership style have on participants?

## Democratic

A **democratic leader** shares power with participants, involving participants in decision making and often asking the group for opinions and ideas.

A democratic leadership style might be useful when leading a group of peers or a team of highly experienced participants. This is because it allows participants to share their expertise and feel that their views are being heard. A good example of democratic leadership in action is a captain of a sports team asking players for ideas on training drills or match tactics. A team huddle is another example of democratic leadership in action, as all the players in a team stand in a circle visibly sharing power.

**B** ronze

**11.** Which famous sports leaders are known for having a democratic leadership style and what effect does their leadership style have on participants?

## Laissez-faire

A **laissez-faire leader** is very hands-off, supplying the venue or equipment and making themselves available for consultation but allowing participants to make their own decisions and solve their own problems.

A laissez-faire leadership style is useful with highly capable, self-motivated participants who need minimal supervision and support. A group that has met regularly for 10 years to play football or tennis once a week might respond well to laissez-faire leadership.

**B** ronze

**12.** Which famous sports leaders are known for having a laissez-faire leadership style and what effect does their leadership style have on participants?

**13.** The benefits of the three leadership styles, and when it is most appropriate to use each of them, have been described. Can you think of any drawbacks of using each leadership style? When would it be inappropriate to use each leadership style?

Regularly participating in sport and physical activity can have huge physical and psychological benefits. Regular exercise can make you fitter and healthier and help you avoid some serious long-term health issues. It can also make you feel less anxious, more self-confident, and more motivated about your life in general, thereby improving your mental health.

## The physical benefits

The physical benefits of participation in sport and physical activity can be divided into short-term benefits and long-term benefits.

**Muscles increase in temperature and become more pliable**

As we exercise, our working muscles get warmer. This increase in temperature happens because heat is released as our muscles convert fuel into the energy we need to move and because of the increase in blood flow to the working muscles. Warmer muscles are more flexible, or 'pliable', than colder muscles. Think of muscles like a piece of chewing gum; the warmer they get, the softer and more flexible they are.

**Oxygen is delivered to your working muscles more quickly and carbon dioxide is removed more quickly**

When you exercise, your rate of breathing (the number of breaths you take in one minute) and your depth of breathing increase, bringing more oxygen into the body and expelling more carbon dioxide. Your heart rate (the number of times your heart beats in one minute) also increases, increasing the speed at which oxygen is transported around your body by your red blood cells. These short-term effects of exercise mean that more oxygen is delivered to your working muscles more quickly, and more carbon dioxide is removed more quickly, and your body is able to work aerobically for longer as a result.

**The short-term physical benefits of participation**

## The range of movement at joints increases

Synovial joints are the most common type of joint in the human body. They allow the bones at the joint to move freely. Your knee joints, hip joints, and shoulder joints are all synovial joints. The ends of the two bones that meet at a synovial joint are covered in slippery hyaline cartilage. The cartilage is lubricated and kept moist by a clear fluid known as synovial fluid, which is secreted from a lining inside the joint capsule.

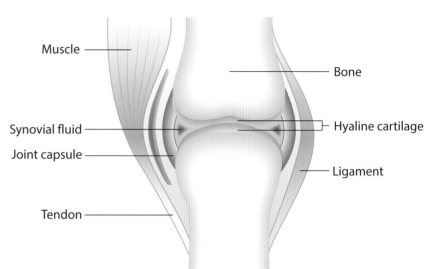

The movement that increases the temperature of your muscles also increases the production of synovial fluid in your synovial joints. This allows your joints to move more freely. As the muscles surrounding the joints are also more pliable, you will experience an increase in the range of movement at your joints during exercise.

## Lactic acid is removed and the cardiovascular system returns to its resting state during a cool-down

Lactic acid is produced when energy is released anaerobically. If lactic acid builds up in our working muscles, we experience pain and fatigue. Once lactic acid has been created, it needs an increased oxygen supply to clear it. This is part of the reason why your heart rate and your rate and depth of breathing remain high for quite some time after physical activity. It is also why a cool-down is important. A cool-down gradually lowers your heart rate and your rate and depth of breathing to their pre-exercise levels.

## B ronze

1. Design and carry out an experiment to investigate one of the short-term physical benefits of participation in sport and physical activity. You could design an experiment that measures heart rate or breathing rate and depth of breathing before, during, and after 10 minutes of physical activity, or you could design an experiment that measures the pliability of muscles before and after exercise.

## Reduced risk of Type 2 diabetes

Insulin is a hormone produced by your body to convert carbohydrates into glucose. It helps the body use the glucose to generate energy immediately or store the glucose so that it can be used to generate energy later. Type 2 diabetes occurs when your body does not produce enough insulin to function properly, or when your body is resistant to the insulin you produce. It can lead to blindness, kidney failure, heart attack, and stroke.

Being overweight is one of the causes of Type 2 diabetes. Consequently, taking part in regular sport and physical activity can reduce your risk of Type 2 diabetes because it helps you maintain a healthy weight. Taking part in sport and physical activity can also help you lower your resistance to insulin and regulate the level of glucose in your blood, by raising your level of insulin sensitivity. The more sensitive to insulin you are, the less you need to regulate the level of glucose in your blood. Physical activity raises insulin sensitivity because more glucose is used to generate energy immediately, which means less insulin is needed to store unused glucose for later use.

The cardiorespiratory benefits

The long-term physical benefits of participation

## Reduced risk of hypertension

If you live an unhealthy lifestyle – eating too much fatty, sugary, and salty food; smoking; drinking alcohol; and doing too little exercise – your blood vessels can become partly blocked with fatty deposits. This makes your blood vessels narrower, making it harder for blood to flow and causing high blood pressure or 'hypertension'. The heart then has to work harder to pump blood around the body, which can lead to other heart-related health problems.

Physical activity, especially aerobic exercise, reduces your risk of hypertension by expanding the blood vessels and increasing the blood flow through them, both of which prevent the fatty deposits forming.

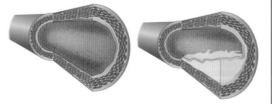

➔ *The image on the left shows a normal blood vessel and the image on the right shows a blood vessel partly blocked with fatty deposits.*

## The heart becomes larger and stronger

As a result of regular aerobic exercise, the heart experiences cardiac hypertrophy. The walls of the heart become more muscular and the heart becomes more efficient, carrying more oxygen to the working muscles with each heartbeat.

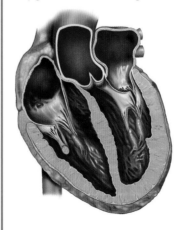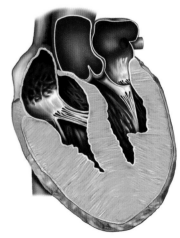

➔ *The image on the left shows a normal heart and the image on the right shows a heart with increased muscle brought about by cardiac hypertrophy.*

## Reduced risk of osteoporosis

People who are not very active do not regularly stress their bones and joints. As a result, their bones become less dense, weaker, and more susceptible to fractures. Eventually they may develop osteoporosis, which is extremely low bone density that results in a very high risk of broken bones. Taking part in regular high-impact exercise stresses your bones and joints, increases your bone density, and reduces your risk of osteoporosis.

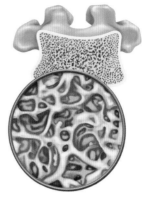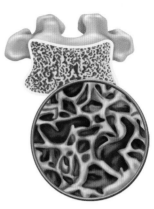

➜ *The image on the left shows normal bone density and the image on the right shows osteoporosis.*

## The musculoskeletal benefits

## Reduced risk of joint injury

Taking part in regular strength training places your ligaments and tendons under stress. In response, they get bigger and stronger and keep your joints much more stable. As a result, people who do not regularly take part in physical activity are more at risk of joint injuries than people who do exercise.

## Increase in flexibility

Regular stretching can improve your flexibility and increase the range of movement at your joints. Carrying out developmental stretches during a cool-down or taking part in activities such as yoga can help you increase your flexibility.

### Link

Remind yourself of the different kinds of stretches that improve flexibility on pages 64–65.

## Reduced risk of poor posture

Spending too much time sitting at a desk or on a sofa watching television can shorten key postural muscles and alter the way we stand. Poor posture creates extra strain on our joints and muscles, which affects the efficiency and quality of our movements and can lead to discomfort and pain. Pilates and yoga are examples of activities that develop core muscle strength and help us avoid poor posture.

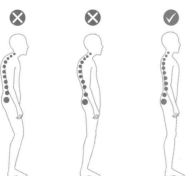

➜ *The two images on the left show poor posture and the image on the right shows good posture.*

> **If exercise were a pill, it would be one of the most cost-effective drugs ever invented.**
> **Dr Nick Cavill**

### B ronze

2.  Create a poster promoting the physical benefits of regular participation in walking football games to older people.

# The psychological benefits

There are psychological benefits to participating in sport and physical activity.

## Increased motivation

Regularly taking part in sport and physical activity can be very motivating. Whether it's extrinsic motivation provided by the leader or intrinsic motivation coming from within, getting active can motivate you to work harder and concentrate more in each session and can keep you coming back week after week.

### Link

Remind yourself about motivation on pages 94–95 and about self-confidence on pages 96–97.

## Increased self-confidence

Regularly taking part in sport and physical activity can help you reach your optimum weight and tone your muscles, making you feel more confident about the way you look. Achieving the sporting targets you have set for yourself or meeting new friends through sport can also increase your self-confidence, and can be the encouragement you need to ensure you continue to participate.

## Experiencing the feel-good factor

Serotonin is a naturally occurring chemical. It helps to regulate your mood and the way you interact with other people. Low levels of serotonin have been linked to depression. Endorphins are hormones that reduce your perception of pain and trigger a positive feeling in the human body.

Exercise, especially aerobic exercise, has been shown to increase both serotonin and endorphins. Taking part in sport and physical activity really does make you happier as well as healthier!

**The psychological benefits of participation**

## B ronze

3. Choose a sport or physical activity that requires a minimal amount of equipment that an adult could take up to improve their psychological well-being. Explain your choice.

## S ilver

4. a) Write down each skill and each quality of a sports leader on a separate piece of paper.

   b) Write down each benefit of participating in sport and physical activity on a separate piece of paper. If you can, use different-coloured paper from the paper you used to write down the skills and qualities of a sports leader.

   c) Which skills and qualities of a sports leader result in which benefits? Match skills and qualities with benefits to find out. You may need to use some benefits more than once; if you do, create more cards.

## G old

5. Which skill or quality of a sports leader is most important? Order the groups of cards you organized for Activity 4, with the most important skill or quality at the top and the least important skill or quality at the bottom. Explain what criteria you used to order the skills and qualities and justify your decisions.

**Learning aim A:** Understand the fundamentals of sport and activity leadership

## Scenario

You are shadowing an experienced sport and activity leader for a week, observing them while they work. They have asked you to write a blog post about what you have learned about the skills and qualities of a successful sports leader and the physical and psychological benefits of taking part in sport and physical activity.

## Task

Write a blog post about the skills and qualities of a successful sports leader, the physical and psychological benefits of participating in sport and physical activity, and how a successful sports leader can help participants experience these benefits. Your blog post should:

**Level 1 PASS**

→ Identify some skills and qualities of a successful leader (A.1P1).
→ Identify some benefits of participating in sport and activity sessions (A.1P2).

**Level 1 MERIT**

→ Outline the skills and qualities needed to be a successful leader (A.1M1).
→ Outline the benefits of participating in sport and activity sessions (A.1M2).

**Level 2 PASS**

→ Explain how successful leaders demonstrate the required skills and qualities (A.2P1).
→ Explain the physical and psychological benefits of taking part in sport and activity sessions (A.2P2).

**Level 2 MERIT**

→ Analyse how a good leader can promote physical and psychological benefits (A.2M1).

**Level 2 DISTINCTION**

→ Evaluate a successful leader and the different ways physical and psychological benefits can be promoted to encourage regular participation (A.2D1).

## Tackling the assignment

Begin your blog by explaining the skills and qualities of a successful sports leader and the physical and psychological benefits of taking part in sport and activity sessions regularly. When you explain something, you need to provide examples or evidence to illustrate your description or provide reasons to tell the reader why it is like it is. It would, therefore, be useful to do some research here, so that you can, for example, provide examples of famous sports leaders exhibiting the skills and qualities you are talking about. Also remember to draw on previous learning, developing your explanation of the short-term and long-term physical benefits of participation by drawing on your understanding of the long-term effects of exercise on the body systems from Component 1, and developing your explanation of the psychological benefits of participation by drawing on your understanding of the psychological influence of motivation and self-confidence on participation from Component 2.

If you are aiming for a Level 2 Merit, you also need to make a link between the skills and qualities of a leader and the physical and psychological benefits of participating by analysing how a leader uses their skills and qualities to help deliver the benefits to participants. When you analyse something, you need to structure your work carefully so that the reader is introduced to each point you want to make in a logical order. You need to provide lots of detail and you need to explore an issue from all angles.

If you are aiming for a Level 2 Distinction, you also need to consider the advantages and disadvantages of each skill and quality a successful sports leader possesses and evaluate which skills and/or qualities have the most impact on helping to deliver the physical and psychological benefits of participation. Remember, when you evaluate something, you need to bring together all the information you have about a topic and review it before reaching a conclusion.

## Meeting the **Level 2 Pass** criteria

### The skill of communication

It is important for a sports leader to demonstrate really good verbal and non-verbal communication skills.

#### Verbal communication skills

A good sports leader will adapt their verbal communication skills to the people taking part in the sport or activity session they are leading. For example, someone leading a session for 12 year olds in a sports hall should speak loudly and clearly because their voice will echo in a large, empty room. They should also make sure they use simple language to make it easier for the children to understand what is required of them. Their tone of voice should usually be warm, unless the young people start to misbehave and then they must use a stricter tone to express their unhappiness with the situation and to re-establish their authority.

Youth team coaches, like football's England Under-18s coach, Neil Dewsnip, have to speak very clearly and loudly when coaching young players because the training field can become a very noisy place. When working with younger players, Dewsnip also uses less technical language than a coach would use with adult players.

> This is a good explanation of verbal communication, which makes reference to tone, volume, and appropriate vocabulary, and how it can be adjusted to meet the needs of different participants.

> It is great to see a real-life example, which illustrates the points already made about the importance of verbal communication.

> This is a strong piece of work so far, and if this learner explains the other skills and qualities of a successful leader, and the physical and psychological benefits of taking part in sport and activity sessions in the same way, they will meet the criteria for a Level 2 Pass.

## Meeting the Level 2 Merit criteria

### Extrinsic motivation and the long-term benefits of participation

A leader can use extrinsic motivation to ensure the participants gain the long-term physical and psychological benefits of taking part in sport and physical activity.

If a sport and activity leader praises participants and ensures that all feedback is phrased positively, they will extrinsically motivate the people attending their sessions. Participants will respond by working harder in each session and by returning to take part week after week.

The sports leader's use of extrinsic motivation will have a direct impact on participants' long-term physical health. They will experience cardiac hypertrophy, lower resting heart rate, and lower resting blood pressure. Their gaseous exchange will become more efficient, their vital capacity will increase, the number of red blood cells in their blood will increase, and their blood will become less viscous. These long-term adaptations to the cardiorespiratory system mean participants will have a reduced risk of Type 2 diabetes and hypertension.

This learner has made a strong link between something a sport and activity leader can do (provide extrinsic motivation) and the way it leads to long-term engagement by participants, who benefit physically and psychologically as a result.

The learner has begun to analyse how a leader who uses extrinsic motivation has an impact on the long-term health of participants. The approach is logical and, if the learner has already met the Level 2 Pass criteria and continues in this way, they should meet the criteria for a Level 2 Merit.

## Meeting the Level 2 Distinction criteria

### Extrinsic versus intrinsic motivation

A sport and activity leader can directly affect participants' extrinsic motivation. This is a real advantage to the leader, who can use praise and positive feedback to encourage participants to return session after session and to work hard. However, there are some disadvantages to relying on extrinsic motivation to keep participants engaged. Because extrinsic motivation comes from the leader, participants do not take ownership of their own motivation and personal development; participants can become over-reliant on their coach to help them achieve their goals.

In contrast, intrinsically motivated participants are much less reliant on their coach. They do not need regular input from their coach and can take responsibility for their own progression. This is generally a very positive thing, but it can be problematic if participants do not push themselves hard enough. In this situation, a coach may need to step in and provide additional extrinsic motivation.

Comparing the two types of motivation, it is evident that both extrinsic and intrinsic motivation play an important role in motivating participants to commit to taking part in sport and physical activity over a long period of time. A sport and activity leader can directly influence a participant's extrinsic motivation but needs to find less direct ways to influence a participant's intrinsic motivation. For example, a well-organized session with a structure that pushes participants to progress will be more enjoyable for participants and should lead to an increase in their intrinsic motivation.

This is a strong evaluation, looking at the advantages and disadvantages of extrinsic and intrinsic motivation and the extent to which a sport and activity leader can encourage extrinsic and intrinsic motivation to deliver long-term physical and psychological benefits for participants.

If the learner has already met the Level 2 Pass and Merit criteria and continues in this way, evaluating other skills and qualities in a similar way and coming to a conclusion about which skill or quality has the biggest impact on participants' physical and psychological health, they will meet the criteria for a Level 2 Distinction.

Participation in sport and physical activity throughout life can be thought of as a journey. At each step along the way, at each stage in life, people require different things from sport and physical activity. Some groups of people – such as disabled people, women, people from different ethnic groups, and lesbian, gay, bisexual, transgender, and intersex people – may also need more encouragement to take part in sport and physical activity to help them overcome barriers to participation. It is the responsibility of sports leaders to ensure that activities are tailored to participants' needs.

**WARNING**

When thinking about target groups, it is important to remember that some people will fit into more than one target group and that some people who may outwardly appear to fit into one specific target group may not behave stereotypically. Grouping people into categories is, nevertheless, beneficial because it can help people planning activity sessions to better tailor them to participants' needs.

## Children and young people

### Primary school-aged children

Engaging in active play helps very young children develop healthy habits that can last a lifetime. It helps them develop agility, balance, and coordination, which together are known as 'physical literacy'. Physical literacy forms the foundation of all sporting skills.

→ *The Lawn Tennis Association invented Mini Tennis Red for children under the age of eight. It is just like tennis, and encourages children to use a range of shots and take part in long rallies. However, it uses a softer ball, which is slower and does not bounce as high as a regular ball and so is easier to hit and control. It also uses shorter rackets and takes place on a smaller court (11m x 5.5m) with a lower net (80cm high). The competitions encourage short, fun matches with tie-break scoring, played as individuals or as part of a team.*

By the time a child starts primary school at around the age of five they will, hopefully, have developed good physical literacy and will be able to take part in recognized sports. However, primary school-aged children, between the ages of 5 and 11, are not yet ready for the physical and mental demands of many sports and so the sports are adapted to suit the needs of the age group. The emphasis is on making the sports fun and easy to pick up, encouraging children to take part and work with others, to develop relevant skills and techniques, and gently introducing them to the tactical elements of the sport.

## Teenagers

Teenagers, young people aged between 13 and 19, have a range of different pressures on their time; as schoolwork becomes more serious and time consuming, they develop a wide range of interests and friendships in and out of school, and they go through puberty. It is, therefore, at this point in their lives that young people tend to make choices about their relationship with sport and physical activity.

Some teenagers choose to take part in sport for fun, trying new sports and physical activities, hanging out with their friends, and meeting new people. Some teenagers devote more time to their sporting development, committing to pursuing excellence in one or more sports. However, while teenagers and young adults represent the most active age group, many young people turn away from sport and physical activity during their teenage years.

➔ *This infographic shows the average number of hours per week young people spend on a range of activities in their free time. To appeal to young people, sport needs to compete with technology!*

### Young people's lives are dominated by technology

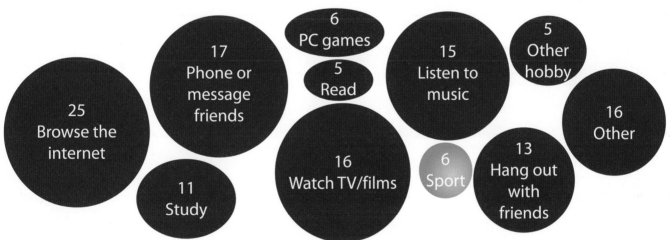

Source: *Sport England,* Youth Insights Pack, *August 2014*

For most sports, teenagers will use the same equipment and follow the same rules as adult participants although some exceptions do exist, to take account of the fact that teenagers' bodies are still growing and strengthening. In cricket, for example, the number of overs a young player can bowl fast in any one spell and over a day is limited, and there are rules around where young players can stand for their own safety. The Rugby Football Union also has strict rules about which age groups are allowed to play and train together to avoid younger, less developed, youngsters playing against, and being injured by, much older and more developed opponents.

## Case study: Josh

I started going through puberty when I was about 13 years old, which I thought was quite late because a lot of the boys I was playing rugby with were getting much bigger than me. I had quite a hard time of it. My parents were splitting up and I had all these changes going on in my body that I couldn't understand. I developed a bit of a short temper and I didn't like the super-competitive nature of playing rugby or the dressing room banter anymore, so I stopped training.

My mum thought I should keep active though and her friend suggested I try out a karate class. I really enjoyed it! It helped me get rid of a lot of energy and think about how to take time to relax and take care of my body. I've enjoyed learning new skills and getting to know a new group of people. We get a lot of guidance and support from the older guys and we all have our own reasons for getting involved.

### Bronze

1. Read Josh's story. Can you identify with any part of his experience? Discuss how puberty affects teenagers and the impact it can have on participation in sport and physical activity.

2. Some sports are being adapted to make them more attractive to teenagers and sports that were relatively unknown 50 years ago are now mainstream.

   a) Find out about Smash Up! from Badminton England. Do you think it will encourage more teenagers to play badminton? Why/why not?

   b) Find out about the evolution of Ultimate Frisbee as a sport. Why do you think it is so popular among teenagers?

## Older people

Older people are people over the age of 65. People experience physical decline as they age and, as a result, older people will generally be less flexible, and will generally have less muscle mass and lower fitness levels than they did when they were younger. Many will also experience some arthritis in their joints; their joints become stiff and painful as the cartilage that helps joints move smoothly is worn away. The number of people participating in sport and physical activity does, therefore, decline with age but many people are keen to carry on exercising and to stay involved in sport and physical activity and many have more free time when they retire. The social aspects of participation, the fun and enjoyment people get from taking part in sport and physical activity, and the health benefits of remaining active all motivate older people to keep exercising.

Some sports are adapted for older participants and many sports have older-age or veteran categories in their leagues so older players can play against people of the same age. For example, walking football is a low-impact form of football that creates less stress on joints as players are not allowed to run, making it perfect for older adults. Many squash players take up racquetball as they get older, because the ball is bouncier, giving players more time to reach it and reducing the stress on their knees. There are also exercise classes specifically designed for older people that are lower intensity and lower impact to avoid placing excess stress and strain on the body.

→ *Two older men play racquetball. Maybe they played squash when they were younger?*

### Bronze

3.  Imagine you are on placement at a local leisure centre. The centre would like to encourage more over-65s to get active, and you have been asked to suggest a programme of sports and physical activities for older adults.

    a) What factors affect the types of activities older people participate in?

    b) Suggest activities, classes, and/or sports that are appropriate for older people, and give reasons for your choices.

# Disabled people

Disability is defined by the government as a physical or mental impairment that has a substantial and long-term negative effect on a person's ability to carry out normal daily activities. Disabilities include visual impairments, hearing loss, and other physical impairments, such as spinal cord injuries or chronic disease, as well as learning disabilities and mental health conditions.

Sport England states that there are now over 9.4 million disabled people in the UK and while participation rates among disabled people are improving, they are still well below the participation rates of non-disabled people. National Governing Bodies are making efforts to ensure sports are accessible to all, but there are a limited number of coaches with the necessary qualifications to deliver disability sports as well as a lack of appropriate facilities.

➜ *Sport England, working in partnership with the English Federation of Disability Sport, which is now called Activity Alliance, has talked to lots of disabled people and has developed these three key ideas to help sports providers understand what disabled people want.*

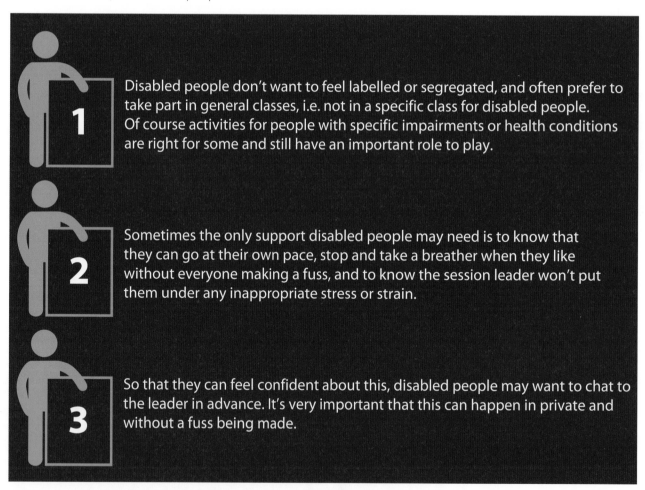

**1** Disabled people don't want to feel labelled or segregated, and often prefer to take part in general classes, i.e. not in a specific class for disabled people. Of course activities for people with specific impairments or health conditions are right for some and still have an important role to play.

**2** Sometimes the only support disabled people may need is to know that they can go at their own pace, stop and take a breather when they like without everyone making a fuss, and to know the session leader won't put them under any inappropriate stress or strain.

**3** So that they can feel confident about this, disabled people may want to chat to the leader in advance. It's very important that this can happen in private and without a fuss being made.

Source: *Sport England and the English Federation of Disability Sport*, Mapping Disability: Engaging Disabled People: the guide, *2016*

## Case study: Megan

I have been registered as severely sight impaired since I was one year old and I attend a specialist school that helps sight-impaired students like myself. I was really inspired by the GB athletes at the Paralympics and wanted to get involved with cycling. I found a session run by some Go-Ride coaches at a specialist disability hub in my county and I was able to try out tandem cycling with a guide partner, who helped me develop my technique, fitness, and confidence. It was important for me to go to a proper session, as my family aren't really cyclists and don't have the ability to guide me, and I was really lucky to find one nearby.

I just love it! The sense of speed and freedom I feel when riding is amazing. I have set myself the goal of taking part in a competition later in the year. My ultimate goal is to be selected for the Paralympic development programme but that's a long way off. I'm just enjoying emulating my heroes at the moment!

## Bronze

4. Jacob and Mae Ling would like to get active. Read their profiles, carry out some research, and recommend at least one sport or physical activity that they could each become involved with. Explain your choices.

> **Jacob** is 25 years old. He is a wheelchair user who is interested in team sports. He has played ball sports in the past, before he began using a wheelchair. He enjoys fast-paced activities and can commit to regular training times at weekends and in the evenings.

> **Mae Ling** is 55 years old. She has rheumatoid arthritis and her joints, particularly her hip joints, are often painful and stiff. She would like to take part in a sport or physical activity that helps improve her flexibility and strength, which she can do while she's away travelling on business.

# Women

Fewer women are involved in sport and physical activity in the UK than men. The media focuses on male sport, at the expense of female sport. This means there is less money in female sport and, consequently, there are fewer opportunities for women to compete at a professional level, fewer girls aspiring to be professional sportspeople, and fewer female role models. Fewer women see sport as a priority in their lives. Not only do women experience fewer opportunities than men to participate once they have left school, but they are also less likely to access the opportunities that are open to them.

However, in recent years, things have begun to change. Recent successes by UK women in rugby, football, cricket, gymnastics, athletics, and hockey have gained good media coverage and there has been an increase in the number of women taking part in these sports as a result. In addition, national campaigns, such as Sport England's 'This Girl Can' campaign, are tackling the outdated idea that exercise is unfeminine and should, therefore, be avoided. This is essential to motivating more women to participate.

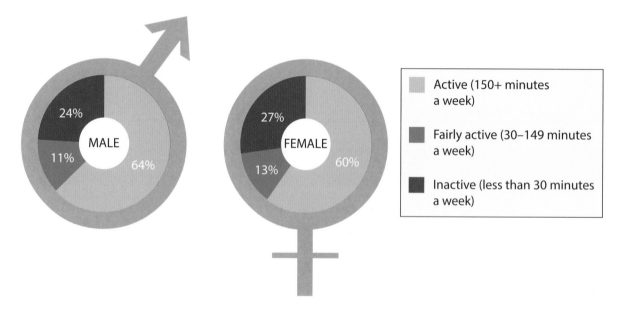

Source: *Sport England*, Active Lives Adult Survey, November 16/17, *March 2018*

→ *This graph shows that men (64% or 14 million) are more likely to be active than women (60% or 13.7 million).*

## B ronze

5. Imagine that you work at a local leisure centre that has a swimming pool and a gym, offers a range of exercise classes, and is home to the local (male) five-a-side football league. Carry out some research and come up with three ideas to make the range of activities on offer at the leisure centre more attractive to women. Explain how each idea will increase participation.

# People from different ethnic groups

An ethnic group is a social group that shares cultural traditions, a religion, a language, or other factors.

Data show that participation in sport and physical activity varies greatly by ethnic group and by gender. Men and women from mixed backgrounds participate most, while women from an Asian background participate least.

Data also show that participation by people from minority ethnic groups is often limited to sports traditionally associated with that ethnic group. This may be because people from minority ethnic backgrounds lack role models they can identify with in other sports. It may also be because National Governing Bodies fail to establish schemes that encourage meaningful participation. While it would appear that minority ethnic groups are well represented in professional sport, this often does not translate into participation at grass-roots level. Furthermore, the number of professional captains, coaches, and managers from minority ethnic backgrounds remains low in most popular sports, fuelling debate about the level of racial discrimination in professional sport.

→ *Cricket is very popular among young people from Caribbean, Indian, and Pakistani backgrounds because of the long-standing tradition of playing the game and the numerous role models in these countries.*

→ *This graph shows participation in sport by ethnic group.*

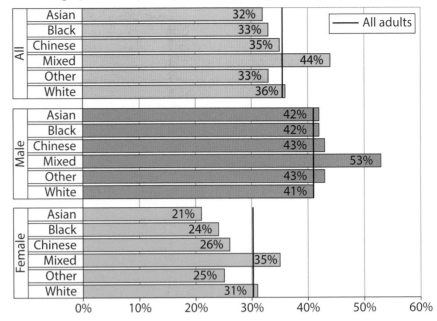

Source: *Sport England,* Active People Survey 6 Q2 (April 2011–April 2012)

## Bronze

6. Mishita would like to get active. Read her profile, carry out some research, and recommend at least one sport or physical activity that she could become involved with. Explain your choice.

> Mishita is 40 years old. When she is asked to identify her ethnic group on a form, she chooses 'Asian'. She looks after her three children, aged 4, 10, and 12, and her elderly mother who also lives with Mishita and her husband. Mishita is overweight and would like to get fitter and healthier but none of her close friends exercise regularly and she doesn't know where to start.

## Lesbian, gay, bisexual, transgender, and intersex people

A report in 2016, from the National LGB&T Partnership and Public Health England, highlighted the fact that lesbian, gay, bisexual, transgender, and intersex (LGBTI) people are less physically active, and over half of all LGBTI people in England were not active enough to maintain good health. The following are some of the reasons LGBTI people give for not taking part in sport and physical activity:

> A lot of the banter that takes place in and around sport and physical activity is homophobic, biphobic, and transphobic. It makes me feel very unwelcome.

> The culture at many sports clubs is very masculine. I am gay and I feel intimidated. I feel I am going to be ridiculed if I try to join in, so I just don't bother.

> I would like to get more involved in sport, but everything is very gendered – the changing rooms, the teams, the competitions – and as a transgender person I just don't want to have to battle my way through it all. It's easier not to get involved in the first place!

> I am gay but none of my teammates know. I keep it a secret from them because I don't know how they will react.

> I'm worried I won't fit in because I'm a lesbian, that I will be made fun of.

Efforts are being made to make sport and physical activity more inclusive and to encourage LGBTI people to get more active, although Sport England is conscious that more needs to be done. Here are some of the things that are making a difference:

→ *Newer sports and physical activities tend to be more attractive to LGBTI people, particularly younger LGBTI people, than traditional sports and physical activities. This is because they are less likely to be associated with a homophobic, biphobic, and transphobic culture and organizational structure. Roller derby has been cited by many lesbians and bisexual women as being particularly welcoming.*

→ People feel more confident about taking part in sport and physical activity if they can see people like them involved in sport at the highest level. This is why LGBTI sporting role models are so important. Tom Daley has won 10 World, Commonwealth, and European gold medals for diving; he came out in 2013. Ryan Atkin is the first openly gay professional football referee.

→ National Governing Bodies (NGBs) play an important role in changing the culture of the sport they manage and Rugby Football League is an example of an NGB that has taken this role seriously. The organization has worked hard over a number of years to gain an insight into the experiences of LGTBI people and to act to make the game more inclusive. For example, it has supported the establishment of an LGBT rugby league club, supported a transgender coach to gain a level two coaching qualification, and issued fines and bans to players using homophobic language.

 **B ronze**

7. Identify a local sports club that you know well and consider what it could do to encourage more lesbian, gay, bisexual, transgender, and/or intersex people to join.

Activity sessions can be roughly divided into three different types: fitness activity sessions, sport activity sessions, and multi-activity sessions. Each type of session appeals to different types of people, with some target groups finding one particular type of session more appealing than the others.

## Fitness activity sessions

**Fitness activity sessions** focus on improving one or more components of fitness, and participants will attend the sessions to achieve personal goals.

→ *These older people are taking part in an aerobics session to improve their aerobic endurance and body composition.*

**⬚ Link**

Look back at pages 51–58 to remind yourself about the components of fitness.

**Types of activity sessions**

## Multi-activity sessions

**Multi-activity sessions** enable participants to try out different sports and physical activities. They can be day-long or week-long, so participants can move from activity to activity, or they can be run over a series of weeks, with participants trying out a different activity each week. They help people find a way of keeping physically active that they enjoy, and stop people getting bored and stuck in a rut by giving them the opportunity to try something they have never tried before.

→ *You might have the opportunity to try out mountain biking, archery, or climbing at a multi-activity session.*

## Sport activity sessions

**Sport activity sessions** are all about participants improving their skills and techniques in a particular sport. Participants may be training to perform competitively, or they may enjoy taking part in a non-competitive environment.

➜ *These wheelchair basketball players are training to compete in a national wheelchair basketball competition.*

## B ronze/Silver

1. Copy and complete the table below to consider how each of the six target groups you have been investigating will respond to each of the three types of activity session.

   Think about what people from each target group will generally like about each type of activity session and what they might not like. Think about the physiological and psychological benefits each type of session offers and the physiological and psychological benefits each target group is seeking. The first box has been filled in for you.

| | Fitness activity sessions | Multi-activity sessions | Sport activity sessions |
|---|---|---|---|
| **Children and young people** | *Children under the age of 13 are too young to take part in fitness activity sessions.*<br><br>*Teenagers may like feeling more confident about their appearance as they get fitter and healthier.*<br><br>*Teenagers may not like the lack of competition that comes with playing a sport; they might get bored and demotivated.* | | |
| **Older people** | | | |
| **Disabled people** | | | |
| **Women** | | | |
| **People from different ethnic groups** | | | |
| **Lesbian, gay, bisexual, transgender, and intersex people** | | | |

In this section you will learn how to plan an activity session, which you will later deliver. It is important that you give your full attention to all areas of the plan and complete a risk assessment, to ensure you are fully prepared for all eventualities and that your activity session is safe, effective, and fun for participants.

## Completing a session plan

When planning an activity session, using a template for a session plan is the best way to ensure that you have thought of everything.

➜ *A template for a session plan.*

| About the participants | | | | | |
|---|---|---|---|---|---|
| Age: | | Number: | | Gender: | |
| Do any of the participants have special educational needs and disabilities (SEND)? If yes, please give details. | | | | | |

| The aim of the session | |
|---|---|
| Target: | |
| Expected outcomes: | |

| About the session | |
|---|---|
| Time: | Location: |
| Resources required: | |

**The session**

**Warm-up**

| Time | Activities | Organization | Teaching points |
|---|---|---|---|
| | | | |

**Main component**

| Time | Activities | Organization | Teaching points |
|---|---|---|---|
| | | | |

**Cool-down**

| Time | Activities | Organization | Teaching points |
|---|---|---|---|
| | | | |

## About the participants

Your session must be planned around the specific needs of the group you are leading. Think about:

### Age

Are your participants primary school-aged children, teenagers, or older adults? Look back at pages 122–125 to help you design a session with activities that are appropriate for the age group you will be working with.

### Gender

Are you working with a group of all male or all female participants, or a mixed group? Differences between genders are relatively small at a younger age but, as they get older, men have the potential to become bigger and stronger than women. It is, therefore, important to consider how different genders will work together in mixed groups and to manage the intensity of the session to get the most out of the participants.

### Participants with special educational needs and disabilities (SEND)

It is important to know if participants have special educational needs, visual or hearing impairments, or other physical disabilities. This enables you to provide the necessary support and to adapt the session to meet their needs if necessary.

### Number

How many participants are you expecting? You will need to make sure that your sport-specific drills and adapted games are suitable for the expected number, and that you have a plan if anyone drops out or if extra people turn up!

You also need to make sure that you have enough leaders to manage the number of participants in the group safely; sports coach UK has rules regarding the ratio of coaches to participants if you are delivering to children and young people. Search for 'Minimum standards for Active Coaches of Children and Young People' on the internet to find out the ratio required for your chosen sport.

### Using personal information appropriately

It is essential for sports leaders to hold personal information about participants. They need to know, for example, if the participant has a disability, a health condition, or learning difficulties and whom to contact if the participant suffers an injury.

The General Data Protection Regulations and the Data Protection Act 2018 are designed to ensure that all those who record and process personal information do so in a fair and lawful manner. This means that sports leaders must make sure the records they hold about participants are accurate and up to date, are kept securely, and are only accessible by approved people. Sports leaders must also keep information that is shared with them more informally confidential, sharing it only if it is appropriate to do so.

### Case study: Adapting games to meet participants' needs

I teach groups from schools across the county and I always make sure that, before I take a group, I understand the needs of each participant so that I can tailor the session accordingly.

I teach football to a group containing a number of kids with hearing loss. The first time I coached them I really struggled to get them to understand the drills. Since then I've really improved my use of hand gestures and body language to get the group's attention, I make sure I give very clear demonstrations, I face the group at all times when I speak, and I always make sure the kids fully understand the drills before we begin. Just taking that little extra care has made a massive difference and I've started learning basic sign language so I can improve even more!

## The aim of the session

The aim of the session is your starting point. Ask yourself: What do I want participants to get out of the session? What do I want participants to be able to do at the end of the session that they could not do at the start of the session? Set yourself a target, what you want to achieve in the session, and then describe your expected outcomes.

You might want participants to focus on improving a weakness that you identified when you observed their performance or you might want them to develop a particular component of fitness. For example:

- Target: To improve passing in basketball
- Expected outcomes: By the end of the session players will be able to confidently use the bounce pass to move the ball past close markers.

- Target: To improve aerobic endurance
- Expected outcomes: By the end of the session participants will be able to complete three rounds of shuttle runs in less than five minutes.

The more specific you can be with targets and expected outcomes, the easier it is to plan a session that delivers them.

## About the session

### Time
How long will the session last for?

### Location
Note the name and location of the facility you will be using. Be specific about the amount of space you need; if using just a quarter of a football pitch, state that. And make sure the facility is booked well ahead of the session.

### Resources
Think through all the resources and equipment you will need to run the session effectively.

Consider the number of balls, nets, cones, and markers you will need, or the protective clothing that participants must wear to take part safely. Make sure you can access everything well before the session to check it is in good condition and has not been damaged. If you need an assistant, note them down as a resource because they will be helping the session run effectively and you will also need to make sure they are available well before the session. Similarly, if you need some technology, such as a tablet with a sports analysis app, note that down too.

## The activities for the warm-up

All activity sessions should begin with a warm-up. A warm-up helps participants prepare physically and mentally for the session ahead, reducing the risk of injury and helping to improve performance. A good warm-up has three stages: pulse raiser, mobilize, and stretch.

### Stage 1: Pulse raiser

Pulse-raising activities, lasting 5–10 minutes, are used to get participants moving and to gently raise their heart rate.

**Football training session warm-up: Pulse-raiser activities**

Travel the width of the pitch and back each time:

- Jog forwards
- Jog backwards
- High knees
- Butt kicks
- Open the gate
- Lunge walking
- Run at 75% of effort
- Sprint at 90% of effort

### Stage 2: Mobilize

Joint mobilization activities involve taking a joint gently through its full range of movement. Effort should focus on the main joints that will be used in the main component of the activity session.

**Joint mobilization activities**

- 10 x shoulder rolls
- 10 x arm circles
- 10 x side bends
- 10 x hip circles
- 10 x quarter squats
- 10 x ankle circles

### Stage 3: Stretch

Stretches performed before exercise should be held for just 6–8 seconds. If you hold them for longer you will lose the benefit of your pulse raiser. Effort should focus on the main muscles that will be used in the main component of the activity session.

Stretches

Abdominals, External obliques, Deltoids, Biceps, Gastrocnemius, Triceps, Adductors, Hip flexor, Gluteus maximus, Hamstrings, Torso, Quadriceps, Hamstrings, Erector spinae

## The activities for the main component

Once participants are warmed up, you can move on to the main component of the activity session. Exactly what this main component consists of will depend on the type of session you are leading.

### Fitness activity session

Fitness activity sessions aim to improve one or more components of fitness. The method of training chosen will depend on the component of fitness the session is designed to improve, but fitness activity sessions tend to utilize gross motor skills, such as walking, running, and jumping, rather than activities involving sport-specific skills.

Exercise classes are a fun way for people to get fitter; exercising alongside others can be more motivating than exercising alone.

→ *A spinning class uses cycling to, primarily, improve aerobic endurance. Other exercise classes develop a range of components of fitness.*

### Link

Look back at pages 51–69 to remind yourself about the components of fitness and the methods of training that improve each component of fitness. You should also consider the principles of training when planning a fitness activity session, and you can remind yourself about the principles of training on pages 70–79.

## Multi-activity session

Multi-activity sessions allow inexperienced participants to have a go at a range of sports and physical activities. These sessions are very interactive and varied, and participants rarely have the time to be bored.

Holiday clubs for children are an example of multi-activity sessions. They are often held at leisure centres, and provide children with opportunities to sign up to a wide range of different activities.

## Sport activity session

Sport activity sessions will include sport-specific drills, to work on improving techniques, and adapted games, to give participants the opportunity to practise techniques in a game context.

### Sport-specific drills

Sport-specific drills are repetitive activities that allow participants to practise particular skills and techniques. They are used by coaches at all levels and, usually, drills get progressively harder throughout the course of a sport activity session. For example:

→ *In this basketball dribbling drill, participants dribble a ball through a series of cones. They dribble the ball using their outside hand, switching hands at each cone. This drill focuses on keeping control of the ball and switching hands sharply.*

→ *In this more advanced basketball dribbling drill, the participant dribbles through staggered cones concentrating on plant and push footwork, staying low with the eyes up, and dribbling in tight spaces before shooting at the basket.*

### Adapted games

Adapted games allow a coach to change the rules of a game to continue to focus on the skills and techniques practised during the drills or to add a fun competitive element at the end of the main component of a sport activity session. They also prepare participants to play a full game. There are two ways that games can be adapted:

1. **Modified games:** Modifying a game allows a coach or a sport activity leader to emphasize a particular game situation. They might alter the number of players on a team or the court or pitch size. For example, to emphasize passing in football, a coach might ask participants to play 4 v 4 in a small space with smaller goals.

2. **Conditioned games:** Placing a condition on a game allows a coach to emphasize a particular skill or technique, often one that has been practised earlier in the session. For example, a table tennis coach who has been teaching a backhand drive might end the session with a game in which he awards an additional point if a rally is won using the backhand drive.

## The activities for the cool-down

It is important to cool down after an activity session. A cool-down gradually reduces the intensity at which participants are working and helps their body systems return to their pre-exercise state. A good cool-down has two stages: pulse lowerer and stretch.

### Pulse lowerer

Activities that gradually lower in intensity, lasting about five minutes, are used to steadily lower participants' heart rates. Activities that involve the large muscle groups used most intensively during the main component of the activity session are best, and you can link them to the main component by involving a ball or slowly rehearsing a movement or tactic you have been practising.

**Football training session cool-down:**
**Pulse-lowering activities**

- Jog at 50% of full pace for 2–3 minutes
- Walk for 2 minutes

### Stretch

It is important to stretch following exercise to reduce the risk of muscle soreness in the days after the activity session by performing **maintenance stretches**. Effort should be focused on the main muscles that were used in the main component of the sport activity session, and stretches should be held for 10–12 seconds.

**Developmental stretches** follow maintenance stretches and are used to lengthen muscles, to improve flexibility, and to increase range of movement. Developmental stretches should be held for 15–30 seconds and can be performed by the participant on their own or assisted by a partner.

**Maintenance stretches**

Abdominals · Biceps · External obliques · Deltoids · Gastrocnemius · Triceps · Adductors · Hamstrings · Hip flexor · Quadriceps · Gluteus maximus · Torso · Erector spinae · Hamstrings

**A developmental stretch for the hamstrings**

## Timing of each activity

Note how much time you will devote to each activity. Generally, it is best to allow 5–10 minutes for the warm-up and 5 minutes for the cool-down, breaking up the main component of the session as required. And don't forget to add up the time allocated to each activity to make sure that it does not exceed the total time allowed for the session!

## Teaching points

Teaching points for each activity should be included where appropriate. These briefly explain the key points you are planning to communicate to participants, to encourage them to perform each activity safely and effectively.

For example, alongside the warm-up activities, you might choose to include teaching points that explain the purpose of each part of the warm-up and teaching points encouraging participants to stretch safely. Alongside the activities in the main component, you might choose to include teaching points that explain correct technique or remind participants how to perform the activity safely.

## Organization

While it is important to list the resources and equipment required for the whole session, it is also helpful to plan which pieces of equipment are needed during each part of the session. This will allow you to think ahead and make sure you are organized, so the equipment you need is ready when you need it and the session runs smoothly.

### Bronze

1. Produce a session plan for a 50-minute netball session for 14 participants, all aged 16. They need to learn how to move the ball effectively among themselves as a team. None of the participants have any special educational needs and disabilities. They play at an intermediate level, competing regularly against other local schools.

### Silver/Gold

2. It is not always enough to simply produce a lesson plan. Often you will be expected to justify your choice of activities.

The key to successfully justifying your decisions is to know your participants. Get as much information as you can about their needs, their ability, and what benefits they are hoping to get out of taking part in the session. You must also be very clear about the aim of your session. All the points you make to justify your choices should reference these elements. Your justification should consider:

- how the activities you have selected for each part of the session link to the type of session and the aim of the session
- how the activities you have selected are appropriate for the participants:
  - why are the activities you have chosen appropriate for the people who will be participating in the session?
  - why are the activities you have chosen appropriate for the ability level of the people who will be participating in the session?
  - what physical and psychological benefits are the participants looking to get out of the session and how will the activities you have chosen deliver these benefits?

Look back at the session plan you produced for Activity 1 and justify your session plan.

# Health and safety

When you lead an activity session, you assume responsibility for participants' health and safety while they are in your care. Although there is always a risk that an accident will happen and someone will get injured, it is important that, as a sports leader, you take steps to minimize the risks by carrying out a risk assessment. You should also make sure participants are aware of any risks before they take part by asking for their informed consent.

 **Link**

When carrying out a risk assessment, think about the causes of common sporting injuries and how they can be prevented (pages 26–29).

## Risk assessment

There are six stages to producing a formal risk assessment document. Failure to comply with any of the six stages could lead to someone being seriously injured.

**(1) Identify the hazards**

Hazards are things that can, potentially, cause harm or injury to a person. Hazards can come from the participants themselves, from equipment, and from the environment. Look around at every part of the facility, the location, and the equipment, think about the participants, and decide what could cause harm, no matter how minor. For example, a piece of broken equipment would be a hazard.

**(6) Review your decisions regularly and make changes if necessary**

Hazards change, so the risk assessment must be reviewed regularly to keep it up to date.

**(5) Record your findings and implement the control measures identified**

By law, the risk assessment must be written down. You can use a risk assessment form to do this. It is also important to put in place the control measures you have decided on.

**(4) Decide how to prevent or reduce the level of risk**

Practical solutions to reduce the level of risk, called 'control measures', must be identified. These can include:

- checking playing surfaces, equipment, and the playing area carefully before activities begin and removing as many potential hazards as possible
- using padding to minimize the impact of collision; for example, padding goalposts or sharp door handles near the playing area
- briefing participants carefully to make sure they understand how to participate safely
- insisting that all participants wear appropriate protective clothing
- having a trained first aider on hand to deal effectively and efficiently with injuries if they do occur.

## Case study: Nadia

I like to get to the training ground before training starts. There are a number of hazards around the pitch that could injure the players and I have to check the pitch and equipment before we start, to ensure we minimize the risk of injury. I walk up and down the pitch, removing water bottles, snack wrappers, and sock tape, which are all trip hazards. I then put pads around the posts and put out the corner flags so players recognize where the edge of the pitch is. Here is an excerpt from my latest risk assessment.

**2 Decide who might be harmed and how**

Decide whether it is the participants, the coaching staff, or any spectators who may be harmed. Then think about what may happen to them and what injuries they may sustain. For example, a broken goalpost could cause a serious head injury to a goalkeeper, or other players nearby, if the goal were to collapse.

**3 Identify the level of risk**

Decide how likely it is that the accidents you have identified will occur. For example, it is very likely that a broken goalpost will collapse because players and the ball will come into contact with it. Consequently, it is high risk. Something that is unlikely to happen, such as a badminton post falling over, is low risk.

### Risk assessment

| Date risk assessment completed | 16 August 2019 | Name of person completing risk assessment | Nadia Marić |
|---|---|---|---|
| Location | Southfields Rugby Training Ground, pitch 2 | | |
| Nature of the activity | Regular rugby union training | | |
| Participants | Under-15 boys first team | | |

| Hazard | Risk | Level of risk | Control measures |
|---|---|---|---|
| Goalposts | Participants will hit the posts and injure themselves | High | Put pads around the goalposts |

## B ronze

3. Look back at the session plan you produced for Activity 1 on page 141 and complete a risk assessment for the session. To help you do this, imagine that the session is taking place in a specific location in your school.

## Informed consent

Participants – or, if they are under 18, the participant's parent or guardian – should complete an informed consent form before taking part in sport and physical activity sessions. This ensures each participant is fully aware of what will take place during the session and of the associated risks, and provides them with an opportunity to withdraw if they are not happy taking the risks highlighted.

An informed consent form should:

- ask participants to provide their personal details (full name, address, telephone number, email address, and emergency contact details)
- explain the target and expected outcomes of the session
- give details of any risks that participants may be exposed to by taking part in the session
- provide participants with an opportunity to disclose any injuries or illnesses that may affect their ability to participate in the session safely
- highlight a participant's right to withdraw from the session at any stage for whatever reason
- include space for the participant to sign and date the form, thereby agreeing to take part in the session based on the information provided above and despite the risks.

 **B ronze**

**4.** Look back at the session plan you produced for Activity 1 on page 141 and design an informed consent form for participants to complete prior to taking part in the session.

 Harstow Rugby Union Club
Main Road, Harstow, BK6 9FD

### Consent Form

Taking part in a rugby union training session brings with it an acceptance of a number of risks. Rugby is a contact sport that can sometimes lead to musculoskeletal injuries. A thorough risk assessment – which is available to view on request – has been carried out, and control measures have been put into place to reduce the likelihood of risks occurring and to reduce the severity of any injuries that arise, but it is not possible to eliminate the risk of injury completely.

A designated first aider is available to participants at all times.

Please complete the following details to consent to taking part in the rugby training session with full awareness of the risks, and to acknowledge that you can withdraw at any time if you wish to.

First name: _____   Surname: _____

Address: _____

_____

Email address: _____

Emergency contact name: _____   Emergency contact telephone number: _____

Relationship of emergency contact to you: _____

Please provide details of any injuries or illnesses that may prevent you from participating safely in the session:

_____

_____

Please list any medication you are taking and the frequency with which you take it:

_____

I agree to take part in rugby training sessions at Harstow Rugby Union Club with the full knowledge of the risks and the measures implemented to control them. I am aware that I can withdraw at any time.

I also agree to inform the sports leader of any accidents or near misses I experience during the session.

Signature: _____   Date: _____

# 3B Practice for Component 3, Learning aim B assignment

**Learning aim B:** Planning sessions for target groups

## Scenario

You have just started work at a local leisure centre, helping coaching staff run activity sessions for a wide range of different participants. You have been given the opportunity to plan and lead a session.

## Task

Prepare a session plan and a risk assessment for an activity session for a target group of your choice, and prepare an informed consent form for participants to complete. Your session plan should be accompanied by a written report justifying the activities you are planning to include in your session. You should:

→ Prepare an outline of an activity session plan for a chosen target group, with support (B.1P3).

→ Prepare a realistic outline of an activity session plan for a target group (B.1M3).

→ Prepare a realistic activity session plan for a chosen target group, explaining choice of activities (B.2P3).

→ Prepare a detailed, realistic, and well-structured activity session plan, giving detailed reasons for suitability for the chosen target group (B.2M2).

→ Produce a comprehensive, realistic activity session plan, giving considered reasons for the activities included and the benefits of participation for the target group (B.2D2).

## Tackling the assignment

Make sure that your session plan, your risk assessment, and your consent form are as realistic as possible. You are going to be delivering the session so make sure you have lots of experience taking part in the type of session you decide to plan. Choose a target group that you know well so that you really understand the physical and psychological benefits the participants are seeking from the session. Finally, plan to run the session somewhere familiar so it is relatively easy to identify real hazards when you do your risk assessment.

The key to successfully completing this assignment is drawing together lots of the things you have learned throughout the course and providing lots of detail in the report you write to accompany your session plan, your risk assessment, and your consent form. The following checklist will help you make sure your report covers everything it needs to cover:

- Have you explained the aim of the session? How does the aim of the session meet participants' needs and encourage them to join in?

- Have you explained why the resources you have listed as required to run the session are important?

- Have you justified each activity you have included in the warm-up? Think about the way in which the warm-up helps the body systems prepare for the physical activity that follows. Remind yourself about the body systems by looking at pages 6–13 and about the short-term benefits of participation in sport and physical activity by looking at pages 114–115.

- Have you justified each activity you have included in the main component? How do the activities you have selected for each part of the session link to the type of session and the aim of the session? How are the activities you have selected appropriate for the participants?

  - Do the activities help participants benefit from the long-term effects of exercise? Remind yourself about the physiological impact of engagement in sport and activity on the body systems by looking at pages 14–17 and about the long-term physical benefits of participation in sport and physical activity by looking at pages 116–117.

  - If you are planning a fitness session, have you chosen an appropriate method of training for the component of fitness you aim to improve? Remind yourself about the components of fitness by looking at pages 51–58 and the methods of training on pages 60–69.

  - If you are planning a fitness session, have you applied the FITT principles and the principles of training to the target group? Remind yourself about the FITT principles and principles of training by looking at pages 70–79.

  - What psychological benefits are the participants looking to get out of the session and how will the activities you have chosen deliver these benefits?

- Have you justified each activity you have included in the cool-down? Think about the way in which the cool-down helps the body systems return to their pre-exercise state. Remind yourself about the body systems by looking at pages 6–13.

# Meeting the **Level 2 Pass** criteria

## The warm-up activities

The warm-up for this football session aimed at young people includes a pulse raiser, mobilizing activities, and stretches.

**Pulse raiser**

The pulse-raiser activities involve moving around the pitch in a range of different ways:

- jogging forwards
- jogging backwards
- high knees
- butt kicks
- open the gate
- lunge walking
- light running
- sprinting.

These pulse-raiser activities are designed to prepare the participant physically and mentally for the session. The initial activities are performed at a moderate intensity and the intensity builds as the warm-up progresses. This allows the participants' heart rate, breathing rate, and depth of breathing to gradually increase, supplying their bodies with the extra oxygen they need. It also allows their muscles to increase in temperature and become more pliable. The activities have been carefully chosen to relate directly to the football session that the participants will be taking part in.

This is a good selection of pulse-raiser activities that are realistic for the target group. However, it isn't clear if participants have to move around the outside of the pitch or travel the length or width of the pitch, and it isn't clear how far they need to travel for each individual activity. If the learner continues in the same way this piece of work would meet the criteria for a Level 2 Pass but more detail is required to meet the criteria for a Level 2 Merit.

The choice of activities has been explained and a link has been made to the sport participants will be taking part in, but to meet the criteria for a Level 2 Merit this learner needs to give detailed reasons why the activities are suitable for the target group and more detail about how each activity prepares participants to take part in a football session.

## Meeting the **Level 2 Merit** criteria

### The warm-up activities

The warm-up for this football session aimed at young people includes a pulse raiser, mobilizing activities, and stretches.

#### Pulse raiser

The pulse-raiser activities involve moving around the outside of the pitch. Participants should move through the list of activities twice:

- jogging forwards (15 seconds)
- jogging backwards (15 seconds)
- high knees (15 seconds)
- butt kicks (15 seconds)
- open the gate (15 seconds)
- lunge walking (15 seconds)
- light running 75% effort (15 seconds)
- sprinting 90% effort (10 seconds).

These pulse-raiser activities are designed to prepare the participant physically and mentally for the session. The initial activities are performed at a moderate intensity and the intensity builds as the warm-up progresses. This allows the participants' heart rate, breathing rate, and depth of breathing to gradually increase, supplying their bodies with the extra oxygen they need. It also allows their muscles to increase in temperature and become more pliable. It is important to include a warm-up at the beginning of a session and to increase the intensity of the activities gradually, because pushing your body too hard straightaway can lead to injury. For example, if you force participants to start by sprinting at 100% effort, then it is highly likely that they will sustain an injury such as a hamstring strain.

The activities in the pulse-raising section of the warm-up have been carefully chosen to relate directly to the football session that the participants will be taking part in. Jogging and sprints replicate movements around the pitch and chasing the ball that may take place during a football match. High knees, butt kicks, open the gate, and lunge walking all prepare participants' joints for the jumps, kicks, and stretches that lie ahead.

The pulse-raiser activities are clearly presented and the timings are realistic for the target group. If the learner continues in the same way and includes an explanation of why the activities are suitable for the target group, this piece of work would meet the criteria for a Level 2 Merit, but more information on the intensity of each activity is required to meet the criteria for a Level 2 Distinction.

This detailed reasoning to justify the suitability of the activities and their intensity demonstrates that the learner is meeting the Level 2 Merit criteria.

# Meeting the Level 2 Distinction criteria

## The warm-up activities

The warm-up for this football session aimed at young people includes a pulse raiser, mobilizing activities, and stretches.

### Pulse raiser

The pulse-raiser activities involve moving around the outside of the pitch. Participants should move through the list of activities twice. The first time, they should work at an average of 9 RPE (very light) and, the second time, they should work at 13 RPE (somewhat hard):

- jogging forwards (15 seconds)
- jogging backwards (15 seconds)
- high knees (15 seconds)
- butt kicks (15 seconds)
- open the gate (15 seconds)
- lunge walking (15 seconds)
- running (15 seconds).

> This is a very realistic set of activities, making use of an RPE scale to monitor intensity.

These pulse-raiser activities are designed to prepare the participant physically and mentally for the session.

The initial activities are performed at a very light intensity and the intensity builds as the warm-up progresses. This allows the participants' heart rate, breathing rate, and depth of breathing to gradually increase, supplying their bodies with the extra oxygen they need. It also allows their muscles to increase in temperature and become more pliable. It is important to include a warm-up at the beginning of a session and to increase the intensity of the activities gradually, because pushing your body too hard straightaway can lead to injury. For example, if you force participants to start by sprinting at 100% effort, then it is highly likely that they will sustain an injury such as a hamstring strain. While a harder warm-up better prepares participants for the demands of the session that follows, there is a higher risk of injury. In contrast, a lighter warm-up minimizes the risk of injury but does not prepare participants' bodies sufficiently for the main event. With this in mind, the pulse-raising activities are designed to be relatively light, with no 100%-effort activities, but also to increase in intensity to prepare the body for what follows.

> This is a very comprehensive justification of the activities included in the pulse-raising phase of the warm-up. If the learner continues in the same way and includes an explanation of why the activities are suitable for the target group and how members of the target group will benefit from the activities this piece of work would meet the criteria for a Level 2 Distinction.

The activities in the pulse-raising section of the warm-up have been carefully chosen to relate directly to the football session that the participants will be taking part in. Jogging and sprints replicate movements around the pitch and chasing the ball that may take place during a football match. High knees, butt kicks, open the gate, and lunge walking all prepare participants' joints for the jumps, kicks, and stretches that lie ahead. These activities will also help prepare participants psychologically for what lies ahead, getting them used to the movements they will be performing later in the session. This reduces the risk of injury during the main component of the session.

It is time to lead the activity session you planned in section 3.B3. Some checklists are provided below, to help you remember everything you need to do. Most important of all, however, is that you relax and have fun. The more you are enjoying yourself, the more participants will enjoy themselves too, because enthusiasm is infectious.

### Before participants arrive

- [ ] Make sure you are dressed appropriately, wearing the right clothing or uniform and footwear for the activity you are leading. You should also have a clean and tidy personal appearance.

- [ ] Make sure you have completed your lesson plan and you have it with you.

- [ ] Collect and check all the equipment you need and make sure any technology you will be using is working.

- [ ] Ensure the facility is appropriate for the session.

- [ ] Put in place all the control methods to reduce the risks you identified in your risk assessment.

- [ ] Check to make sure there are no additional hazards (hazards you have not already identified in your risk assessment). If there are, decide who might be harmed and how, identify the level of risk, decide how to prevent or reduce the level of risk, and implement any control measures identified.

### When participants first arrive

- [ ] Introduce yourself and welcome participants to the session.

- [ ] Check participants' ability and ask them if they have any injuries or medical conditions you need to be aware of.

- [ ] Tell participants about the emergency procedures at the sports facility you are using. Let participants know if there are any fire drills planned and draw their attention to the emergency exits and, if you have to evacuate, the muster points. It is also good to let people know where to get first-aid help should you be unable to assist and where the nearest first-aid room is.

- [ ] Tell participants the target and expected outcomes for the session. This helps them understand what you are trying to achieve and means they are more engaged and motivated.

## During the session

☐ Follow your session plan to meet your set target and expected outcomes, but adapt it if you notice participants finishing activities quickly and getting bored or struggling to complete activities in the allotted time. You may also need to adapt your session plan if equipment is broken, you have more or fewer participants than you were expecting, or if one or more participants have specific needs that you did not know about.

☐ Be organized, thinking one step ahead, to make sure that the session runs smoothly and participants are not hanging around doing nothing while you set something up.

☐ Demonstrate appropriate leadership skills for the activity and participants. Look back at pages 106–109 to remind yourself of what these are.

☐ Demonstrate the qualities of a sports leader. Look back at pages 110–111 to remind yourself of what these are.

☐ Provide accurate demonstrations of each activity, along with clear instructions about how each activity should be carried out.

☐ Provide participants with teaching points where possible.

☐ Observe all participants' technique, moving around the activity area to make sure you can observe everyone clearly.

☐ Provide timely feedback to participants where appropriate.

☐ Monitor participants' health and safety throughout the session.

## After the session

☐ Give participants feedback on how they have performed in relation to the target and expected outcomes of the session.

☐ Give participants the opportunity to give you feedback, reflect on the session, and ask questions.

☐ Follow the correct procedures for checking and putting away the equipment you have used.

☐ Make sure the facility is left in an acceptable condition for the next session.

### B Bronze/Silver/Gold

1. Use the checklists above to help you lead the main component of the activity session you planned in section 3.B3.

Personal development should be a priority for all sports leaders. The best coaches in the world reflect on each session they deliver, thinking about what worked well and what did not work so well, and using their findings to influence the planning and delivery of future sessions. They 'Plan Do Review'.

There are five parts to a successful review:

### Self-reflection

The first step involves reflecting on how you think your planning and leading went. Ask yourself the following questions:

- Did the planned activities support the target and expected outcomes of the session? Why/why not?
- Did the planned activities meet the needs of the participants? Why/why not?
- How well did the session itself meet the intended target and expected outcomes?
- How well did the session itself meet the needs of the participants?
- What went well in the session and why?
- What did not go so well in the session and why?

For example:

The technology did not work as I had hoped. Two of the heart rate monitors didn't work properly. I tried to think on my feet and asked people to share, but it meant that part of the session took longer than expected and we ran out of time towards the end of the session as a result.

The circuit training session was designed to focus on developing muscular endurance, which is the component of fitness participants were expecting to work on improving. The participants all had different levels of muscular endurance, and it was straightforward to modify the number of repetitions of each exercise required and the rest periods between exercises to meet the individual needs of each participant.

## ② Reviewing feedback gathered

You can gather feedback from participants and from supervisors to give you additional perspectives on how the session went. Feedback from participants will probably be quite generalized and will help you get a general sense of what it felt like to take part in the session. In contrast, feedback from supervisors should be a lot more detailed, focusing on specific aspects of your performance. Always try to gather as much feedback as you can, because all feedback – positive and negative – will help you develop as a sports leader.

### Gathering feedback from participants

At the end of a session, if participants do not have to rush off somewhere, you can ask them to give you informal feedback. You can ask them what they liked about the session and what could be improved, and you can note down their feedback when they have gone. Remember that feedback is a gift. You may agree or disagree with the feedback people give you, but always thank people for their feedback and reflect on it, actioning any improvements if necessary.

If you think participants might be reluctant to speak honestly with you, something many people find very difficult, you could ask them to complete a brief, anonymous questionnaire or comments card such as the example shown here.

How far do you agree with these statements on a scale of 1–5, with 1 being 'definitely don't agree' and 5 being 'definitely agree'?

|  | | | | | |
|---|---|---|---|---|---|
| The leader was welcoming | 1 | 2 | 3 | 4 | 5 |
| The target and expected outcomes of the session were clearly communicated | 1 | 2 | 3 | 4 | 5 |
| I enjoyed the warm-up | 1 | 2 | 3 | 4 | 5 |
| I enjoyed the activities in the main component | 1 | 2 | 3 | 4 | 5 |
| I enjoyed the cool-down | 1 | 2 | 3 | 4 | 5 |
| The leader communicated clearly and effectively | 1 | 2 | 3 | 4 | 5 |
| The leader clearly demonstrated techniques | 1 | 2 | 3 | 4 | 5 |
| The leader was attentive and gave lots of feedback and encouragement | 1 | 2 | 3 | 4 | 5 |
| My individual needs were met | 1 | 2 | 3 | 4 | 5 |
| I got what I wanted out of the session | 1 | 2 | 3 | 4 | 5 |

Do you have any other comments?

_____

_____

It can be difficult to gather meaningful feedback from younger participants, so you could ask parents or guardians to fill out comments cards on behalf of children, or encourage parents and guardians to speak with you after the session to share their thoughts about how it went.

### Gathering feedback from supervisors

A supervisor – usually a teacher or a senior coach – might observe your activity session and give you feedback on all aspects of planning and leading. Or, if they are not able to watch the session live, you could video it to discuss what went well and what did not go so well with your supervisor afterwards.

## ③ Identifying strengths

Identifying strengths is really important. When you know what you are doing well, you can make sure you keep doing it. Look at the notes you made while you were reflecting on how you thought your planning and leading went and look at the feedback you received from participants and supervisors. What went particularly well? What are your strengths?

### B ronze

1. **a)** Create a form that you can use to record your observations of how effectively an activity session is planned and led.

   **b)** Observe an activity session and use your form to record your observations.

### 4 Identifying areas for improvement

Identifying areas for improvement is essential if you want to be the best sports leader you can be. Look at the notes you made while you were reflecting on how you thought your planning and leading went and look at the feedback you received from participants and supervisors. What did not go so well? What could you improve on?

### 5 Identifying actions and targets for improvement

Once you have identified your strengths and areas for improvement it is important to set out what actions need to be taken to improve for next time, so that the next session you lead is even better. SMART targets (see page 109) are a really effective way of clearly setting out what you intend to do and by when.

For example:

> My supervisor pointed out that I was not dressed appropriately. Next time I will wear appropriate clothing and footwear for the session I am leading, so that I model appropriate clothing and footwear for participants.

### B ronze/Silver/Gold

2. Reflect on the way you planned and led an activity session:

   a) Describe your strengths and areas for improvement.

   b) Explain the impact your strengths and areas for improvement may have had on the session.

   c) Identify the actions you need to take to improve for next time and set yourself targets for improvement using the SMART target-setting technique.

   d) Annotate your session plan to show what you would do differently next time, explaining the reasoning behind each decision you make.

   e) Justify how the planning and leading of future activity sessions may be impacted positively if you meet your targets for improvement.

   When you justify something, you need to give reasons or evidence to support your opinion. In this case, you need to show how meeting your targets for improvement will lead you to deliver better activity sessions in the future.

## Adding a wider dimension to your review

When an experienced sports leader reviews a session they will look beyond the planned session itself. They will not only consider how the actual session met the target and expected outcomes of the planned session and met the needs of participants; they will also consider whether the session fulfilled a range of other, broader criteria. They will consider whether the session contributed to the overall health and well-being of the participants:

- Did participants experience the short-term benefits of taking part in sport and physical activity during the session? Look back at pages 114–115 to remind yourself of what these are.
- Will taking part in the session have contributed towards participants experiencing the long-term benefits of taking part in sport and physical activity? Look back at pages 116–117 to remind yourself of what these are.
- Did participants experience the psychological benefits of taking part in sport and physical activity during the session? Look back at page 118 to remind yourself of what these are.

An experienced sports leader may also consider whether or not they can provide participants with advice on improving their health and well-being. For example, they may give a participant guidance on how to improve their diet, providing them with a fact sheet on eating a more balanced diet or sharing information on when to eat to maximize sporting performance.

**G** old

3. Evaluate how effectively the activity session you led, and subsequently reviewed, contributed to the overall health and well-being of participants.

# 3C Practice for Component 3, Learning aim C assignment

**Learning aim C:** Delivering and reviewing sessions for target groups

## Scenario

You have just started work at a local leisure centre, helping coaching staff run activity sessions for a wide range of different participants. You have been given the opportunity to plan and lead a session.

## Task

Lead the main component of the activity session you planned for Component 3 Learning aim B. Make sure you collect feedback on the session from participants and supervisors. Then prepare a report reviewing the way you planned and led the session, considering your strengths and the areas you need to work on. You should:

**Level 1 PASS**
→ Lead a component of a sport/activity session with supervision, demonstrating limited application of leadership skills and qualities (C.1P4).
→ Identify own application of leadership attributes with examples (C.1P5).

**Level 1 MERIT**
→ Lead the main components of a planned sport/activity session with supervision, demonstrating some appropriate skills and qualities (C.1M4).
→ Review the planning and leading of the main component of a planned sport/activity session, identifying strengths and areas for improvement (C.1M5).

**Level 2 PASS**
→ Independently lead the main component of a planned sport/activity session, demonstrating use of appropriate skills and qualities throughout (C.2P4).
→ Review the planning and leading of the main component of a sport/activity session, describing strengths and areas for improvement and suggesting targets for future sessions (C.2P5).

**Level 2 MERIT**
→ Discuss own delivery of planned sport/activity session, explaining strengths and areas for improvement and explaining targets for future sessions (C.2M3).

**Level 2 DISTINCTION**
→ Evaluate the delivery of the planned sport/activity session including links to physical and psychological benefits, justifying areas of improvement for future sessions (C.2D3).

## Tackling the assignment

Before you lead the main component of your activity session, consider how you will collect feedback from participants and supervisors. Do you need to create a questionnaire or comment card for participants to complete at the end of the session?

Try not to be nervous during the activity session. Do your very best, and remember that getting things wrong gives you plenty of scope to identify areas for improvement in your review presentation. Remember to collect feedback from participants and your supervisors at the end of the session.

Your presentation should bring together your own thoughts about how the session went with the feedback from participants and supervisors, and consider your strengths and areas for improvement:

- If you are aiming for a Level 2 Pass, you should describe your strengths and areas for improvement. When you <u>describe</u> something, you give a clear account of it in your own words.
- If you are aiming for a Level 2 Merit, you should explain your strengths and areas for improvement. When you <u>explain</u> something, you need to provide examples or evidence to illustrate your description or provide reasons to tell the reader why it is like it is.
- If you are aiming for a Level 2 Distinction, you should evaluate your strengths and areas for improvement and justify your targets for improvement. When you <u>evaluate</u> something, you need to bring together all the information you have about a topic and review it before reaching a conclusion. When you <u>justify</u> something, you need to give reasons or evidence to support your opinion.

If you are aiming for a Level 2 Distinction, you should also add a wider dimension to your review, evaluating how successfully your activity session provided participants with the physical and psychological benefits of taking part in sport and physical activity.

## Meeting the **Level 2 Pass** criteria

Following my session, I asked all participants and my supervisor to complete feedback questionnaires. The questionnaires revealed the following strengths and areas for improvement.

### Strengths

One strength was that the session was well organized. I managed to stick to the timings in my session plan, without the session feeling rushed. All the equipment was ready just before it was needed, so that participants were not standing around doing nothing at any point. I also had enough equipment for all the participants, even though two more than I expected turned up.

Questionnaires completed by participants and supervisors are effective forms of feedback. It is a good idea to submit the completed questionnaires along with your report, to demonstrate how well you have taken on board the feedback you received.

## Areas for improvement

One area for improvement was that the session did not provide very much intrinsic motivation for the participants because it was not particularly fun or enjoyable. I focused so much on being organized that I forgot to be enthusiastic and encourage participants to have fun. In future, I would make a session more fun by incorporating some games into the main component.

## Meeting the **Level 2 Merit** criteria

Following my session I asked all participants and my supervisor to complete feedback questionnaires. I also recorded the session. Reviewing this feedback and thinking about the session myself revealed the following strengths and areas for improvement:

### Strengths

One strength was that the session was well organized.

I managed to stick to the timings in my session plan, without the session feeling rushed. I carefully thought through how long each activity should take when I was writing the session plan, and I kept an eye on my phone throughout to make sure we didn't overrun. The first activity of the main component took slightly longer than expected, because it took longer to put out the cones than I thought it would, but I made up the time during the second activity by reducing the number of times participants moved up and down the pitch.

All the equipment was ready just before it was needed, so that participants were not standing around doing nothing at any point. I also had enough equipment for all the participants, even though two more than I expected turned up. I was only able to be this prepared because I turned up early for the session and made sure everything was in place before the participants arrived.

### Areas for improvement

One area for improvement was that the session did not provide very much intrinsic motivation for the participants because it was not particularly fun or enjoyable. For example, the main component contained a number of sport-specific drills but they did not lead to an adapted game. As a result the participants did not get to put their skills into practice and experience the progress they had made in a game situation and left without the sense of achievement that is an important part of feeling intrinsically motivated. I also focused so much on being organized that I forgot to be enthusiastic and encourage participants to have fun. You can see in the recording of the session that I don't smile very much! In the future, I could make the sessions more fun by incorporating some games into the main component. For example, I could include a five-a-side round robin tournament.

This learner has clearly described one strength and one area for improvement. Notice how their description of the area for improvement is in two parts: they have described what happened and they have described how they would do things differently next time to ensure the session is better. If the learner continues in this way, describing more strengths and areas for improvement, they will meet the criteria for a Level 2 Pass.

This learner is discussing the same strength and area for improvement as the learner who meets the Level 2 Pass criteria, but this learner has explained not described. The highlighted text shows where they have included examples that expand their description. If the learner continues in this way, they will meet the criteria for a Level 2 Merit.

## Meeting the Level 2 Distinction criteria

Following my session I asked all participants and my supervisor to complete feedback questionnaires. I also recorded the session. Reviewing this feedback and thinking about the session myself revealed the following strengths and areas for improvement.

## Strengths

One strength was that the session was well organized.

My supervisor praised the way I managed to stick to the timings in my session plan. I think I achieved this because I carefully thought through how long each activity should take when I was writing the session plan, and I kept an eye on my phone throughout to make sure we didn't overrun. The first activity of the main component took slightly longer than expected, because it took longer to put out the cones than I thought it would, but I made up the time during the second activity by reducing the number of times participants moved up and down the pitch. It is important to be flexible during a session, because things never go exactly to plan, but having the plan allowed me to work out where I could save time when the first activity overran.

Participants also told me that the session did not feel rushed. They said that the pace of the session was good and they were pleased they were always doing something. I think they felt this way because all the equipment was ready just before it was needed, so that participants were not standing around doing nothing at any point. I also had enough equipment for all the participants, even though two more than I expected turned up. I was only able to be this prepared because I turned up early for the session and made sure everything was in place before the participants arrived. It was very easy to make sure I had everything I needed because I just worked through my plan and collected everything together.

## My session and the physical benefits of participation

The session delivered short-term physical benefits to participants which, if they continue to exercise, will lead to long-term physical benefits.

The first benefit was that the session raised participants' heart rates during the pulse-raiser part of the warm-up and maintained a higher than normal heart rate throughout the main component. During the pulse raiser, participants were required to move around the outside of the pitch carrying out a range of different exercises including jogging, sprinting, and butt kicks. The intensity of the exercises increased as the pulse raiser continued and, by the end, participants' heart rates had increased enough to ensure they were receiving enough oxygen and removing enough carbon dioxide quickly enough to enable participants to continue to work mainly aerobically during the main component. Regularly increasing your heart rate like this leads to cardiac hypertrophy. Your heart gets bigger and stronger and your risk of cardiovascular diseases, such as hypertension, is reduced.

This learner is discussing the same strength as the learner who meets the Level 2 Merit criteria, but this learner has evaluated not explained. The highlighted text shows where they have shared the evidence that has led them to their conclusion, and where they summarize the point they are making.

If this learner continues to evaluate their strengths in this way, and then goes on to justify the areas for improvement they have identified, they will meet the criteria for a Level 2 Distinction.

This learner has begun to evaluate how their session provided participants with the physical and psychological benefits of taking part in sport and physical activity. If they continue in this way, evaluating a range of physical and psychological benefits and making links between the short-term benefits of taking part in the session itself and the long-term benefits of regular participation in sport and physical activity, they will meet the criteria for a Level 2 Distinction.

# Glossary

**adaptation** a physical change that makes a body system more efficient

**aerobic endurance** a measure of the body's ability to release energy aerobically, to deliver oxygenated blood to the working muscles, and to remove waste products such as carbon dioxide and lactic acid

**anxiety** the level of nervousness or worry that a participant experiences

**autocratic leader** has absolute power, making all the decisions and imposing these decisions on their group

**blood pressure** the pressure that blood leaving the heart exerts on your arteries

**body composition** a measure of the percentages of fat, muscle, bone, water, and vital organs that make up your body weight

**bone density** the thickness and strength of bones

**bruise** a basic sporting injury that occurs when capillaries rupture and bleed beneath the skin

**calories** energy is measured in calories (kcal); the recommended daily allowance of calories is 2500kcal for an adult male and 2000kcal for an adult female

**carbohydrate loading** eating more carbohydrates than normal before competition or training to ensure the body has the energy it needs to perform

**carbohydrates** the body's main source of energy; divided into simple carbohydrates and complex carbohydrates

**cardiac hypertrophy** the walls of the heart become more muscular and the heart becomes more efficient as a result

**cardiorespiratory system** the name given to the body system that combines the cardiovascular system and the respiratory system

**cardiovascular system** the name given to the body system that pumps oxygenated and deoxygenated blood around the body. It consists of the heart, the blood vessels (the arteries, veins, and capillaries), and the blood

**cognitive anxiety** anxiety that has a psychological effect on the mind

**complex carbohydrates** release energy over a much longer period of time than simple carbohydrates; found in pasta, rice, bread, cereals, oats, and potatoes

**dehydrated** when your body does not contain enough water for it to function as efficiently as it should

**democratic leader** shares power with participants, involving participants in decision making and often asking the group for opinions and ideas

**deoxygenated blood** blood containing a low concentration of oxygen

**developmental stretches** performed to lengthen muscles; should be held for 15–30 seconds

**diffusion** when molecules move from an area of higher concentration to an area of lower concentration in an attempt to reach a balance

**dislocation** a complex sporting injury that occurs when the bones at a joint are displaced

**essential amino acids** the eight amino acids that must be supplied by the food you eat because your body cannot make them itself

**extrinsic motivation** sources of motivation that come from outside a person

**extrovert** a confident and outgoing person who enjoys socializing and is generally very comfortable in other people's company

**fats** important as a source of energy, for transporting fat-soluble vitamins around the body, and certain fatty acids are vital for good health; divided into saturated fats and unsaturated fats

**fibre** helps your body absorb vital nutrients and remove waste products by providing the bulk that is needed to move them through your digestive system; found in carbohydrates and vegetables

**fitness activity sessions** activity sessions that focus on improving one or more components of fitness

**FITT principles** these are applied to a training programme to ensure that training is optimized for success. FITT stands for Frequency, Intensity, Type, and Time

**flexibility** the ability to move your joints through their full range of motion smoothly

**fracture** a complex sporting injury that occurs when a bone cracks or breaks. There are three types of fracture: stress fractures, open fractures, and closed fractures

**gaseous exchange** oxygen moves from the air in the alveoli into the blood in the capillaries. At the same time, carbon dioxide moves from the blood in the capillaries to the air in the alveoli

**heart rate** the number of times your heart beats per minute

**hydrated** when you have enough water in your body for it to function properly

**hypertrophy** the tension, fatigue, and damage caused by strength training prompt muscle fibres to grow larger and stronger

**intrinsic motivation** sources of motivation that come from within a person

**introvert** a shy person who is generally happy in their own company

**joint** an area in the body where two or more bones meet

**lactic acid** a waste product produced when the body releases energy anaerobically

**laissez-faire leader** very hands-off, supplying the venue or equipment and making themselves available for consultation but allowing participants to make their own decisions and solve their own problems

**ligament** connective tissue that connects bone to bone. Ligaments hold a joint together and make it more stable

**macronutrients** nutrients that you need to eat in large quantities; carbohydrates, fats, and protein

**maintenance stretches** performed to reduce the risk of muscle soreness in the days after physical activity; should be held for 10–12 seconds

**micronutrients** nutrients that you need to eat in smaller quantities; includes vitamins and minerals

**motivation** a combination of the internal mechanisms and external stimuli that arouse and direct behaviour

**multi-activity sessions** activity sessions that enable participants to try out different sports and physical activities

**muscular endurance**  a measure of how long a performer's muscles can powerfully contract repeatedly before they suffer fatigue. It relies on the body's ability to deliver oxygen and remove lactic acid

**muscular system**  the name given to the body system that involves the muscles

**musculoskeletal system**  the name given to the body system that combines the muscular system and the skeletal system

**non-essential amino acids**  the 14 amino acids that the body can make itself

**overtraining**  occurs when a performer trains too hard and does not give themselves enough time to rest and recover between training sessions; one of the principles of training

**oxygenated blood**  blood containing a high concentration of oxygen following gaseous exchange at the lungs

**oxygen intake**  taking air from the atmosphere, which contains oxygen, into the lungs when we inhale. As exercise intensity increases, breathing rate increases to increase oxygen uptake

**oxygen uptake**  oxygen from the air in the alveoli diffuses into the capillaries. As exercise intensity increases, oxygen uptake increases as the working muscles demand more oxygen to fuel their contractions

**participant differences and needs**  a training programme must be designed with these in mind; one of the principles of training

**platelets**  a component of blood that enables blood to clot

**power**  the ability to combine strength and speed

**PRICE**  an acronym to describe a method for treating sprains and strains. It stands for Protect, Rest, Ice, Compression, Elevation

**principles of training**  these ensure that training is effective and leads to the adaptations that bring about improvements in performance. The principles of training are: specificity, participant differences and needs, progressive overload, overtraining, reversibility, and training zones

**progressive overload**  gradually increasing a participant's training workload in order for the body to continue to improve through overload (overload takes place when a greater than normal stress is placed on the body, causing adaptations to occur); one of the principles of training

**protein**  provides the body with amino acids; essential for muscle growth and repair; found in chicken, turkey, lean beef, fish, eggs, beans, nuts, seeds, and non-meat protein substitutes such as Quorn™

**rehabilitation**  the process of restoring someone to full health after any injury

**respiratory system**  the name given to the body system that enables breathing, bringing oxygen into the body and expelling carbon dioxide

**reversibility**  adaptations made as a result of training will be reversed if training stops; one of the principles of training

**SALTAPS**  an acronym to describe the steps that should be taken to assess an injury. It stands for Stop play, Ask, Look, Touch, Active movement, Passive movement, Stand up

**saturated fats**  typically solid at room temperature; increase the total amount of cholesterol in your blood, increasing your risk of coronary heart disease; found in fatty meat, cheese, and butter, as well as cakes, crisps, and biscuits

**self-confidence**  the belief that a desired behaviour can be performed

**shin splints**  a complex sporting injury that is characterized by pain in the lower leg. It is an overuse injury

**simple carbohydrates**  provide a quick burst of energy; found in sweets, honey, fruit and fruit juice, chocolate, as well as many snacks and glucose energy drinks

**skeletal system**  the name given to the body system that involves the bones

**somatic anxiety**  anxiety that has a physical effect on the body

**specificity**  choosing methods of training that develop the appropriate components of fitness for the performer's chosen sport or physical activity; one of the principles of training

**speed**  the rate at which an individual is able to perform a movement or cover a distance

**sport activity sessions**  activity sessions that focus on improving skills and techniques in a particular sport

**sprain**  a basic sporting injury that occurs when a ligament twists beyond its normal range

**state anxiety**  temporary anxiety that is brought on by specific high-pressure situations

**strain**  a basic sporting injury that occurs when a muscle or tendon is stretched beyond its normal range

**strength**  the amount of force muscles can generate to overcome resistance

**tendon**  connective tissue that attaches muscle to bone

**tendonitis**  a complex sporting injury that occurs when tendons become inflamed at a joint. It can be an overuse injury

**torn ligament**  a complex sporting injury that occurs when a ligament tears

**training zones**  it is important to work in the appropriate training zone to achieve the required fitness improvements; one of the principles of training

**trait anxiety**  a personality characteristic; a fixed or relatively permanent form of anxiety

**Type A**  a Type A personality is impatient, time-conscious, competitive, outgoing, aggressive, driven, forceful, focused, and rushed

**Type B**  a Type B personality is patient, relaxed, lazy, tolerant, easy-going, calm, passive, stress-free, and laid-back

**unsaturated fats**  normally liquid at room temperature; play a role in reducing your risk of developing coronary heart disease and the body's second source of energy, after carbohydrates; found in oily fish, avocados, almonds, walnuts, and pumpkin seeds as well as oils such as olive oil

**vasoconstriction**  the narrowing of blood vessels to reduce blood flow

**vasodilation**  the widening of blood vessels to increase blood flow

**vital capacity**  the maximum amount of air we can breathe out following a maximum breath in

# Index

stretches 64–5, 117, 137, 140
sumo wrestlers 58
sunburn 27
supplements 90, 92
sweating 87
synovial fluid 87, 115

target groups 122–31
    disabled people 126–7
    ethnic groups 129
    LGBTI people 130–1
    older people 125
    women 128
    young people 122–4
target-setting 33, 80, 97, 109
team talks 99
technology 39–49, 123
    artificial pitches 43
    benefits/limitations 45–6
    clothing 41
    data collection 44–6
    equipment 39–40
    footwear 42
    practice assignment 47–9
    rehabilitation 34–5
    skills analysis 44, 45, 46
temperature regulation 9
    see also body temperature
tendonitis 25, 37
tendons 12, 17, 23, 25, 37, 38, 115
tennis 39, 49, 122
tennis elbow 25
tests
    1-minute sit-up test 53
    12-minute run test 52, 59
    30-metre sprint test 55
    hand grip dynamometer test 56
    sergeant jump test 57
    sit-and-reach test 54
thiamine 85

torn ligament 25
Townsend, Joe 95
training 70–82
    aerobic endurance 60–1, 78
    aims/objectives of 81
    circuit training 62
    continuous training 60, 77
    core stability training 63
    duration of 78, 81
    Fartlek training 61
    FITT principles 70–9
    flexibility training 64
    frequency 73
    goal-setting 80
    injury risk 29
    intensity 74–7
    interval training 60, 66, 77
    medical issues 80
    methods 60–9
    muscular endurance 62–3, 78
    overtraining 70, 73, 79
    participant differences and needs 70, 72, 80
    person-centred approach 80
    planning 80–1
    plyometrics 78
    power training 68–9
    progressive overload 70, 73
    reversibility principle 70, 79
    safe practice 81, 99
    specificity 70, 71
    speed training 66
    sprint training 66
    strength training 16, 67, 78
    stretches 64–5
    training partners 97
    training zones 70, 74–5
    weight training 67
        see also activity sessions

trait anxiety 98
trampolining 28
triceps 10, 64
Type 2 diabetes 116
Type A and Type B personalities 111

unsaturated fats 84
urine 87

valves, heart 6, 7
VAR (Video Assistant Referee) 46
vasoconstriction 9
vasodilation 9
veins 6, 7
verbal communication 106, 120
vertebral column 11
Video Assistant Referee (VAR) 46
video-analysis software 44, 45, 46
visualization technique 33
vital capacity 14
vitamins 85, 92

warm-ups 22, 28–9, 81, 137, 141, 147–9
water 87, 90
waterproof materials 42
wearable technology 44, 45
weather conditions 27
weight-lifting 16, 18, 28, 39, 67
white blood cells 13
whole-body cryotherapy 34
women 128

yoga 32, 117
young people
    age categories 28, 29
    participation 122–4, 139

# Acknowledgements

We are grateful to authors and publishers for permission to use extracts from their titles and in particular for the following:

**Dr N. Cavill:** quote (date unknown). Reproduced with permission from Dr N. Cavill.

**BTEC:** Normative fitness testing data. *Teaching PE & Sport Update*, 21 September 2017 (Pearson Education, 2017). Reproduced with permission from Pearson Education Ltd.

**England Professional Rugby Injury Surveillance Project Steering Group**. *England Professional Rugby Injury Surveillance Project: 2017–2018 Season Report* (Rugby Football Union, 2018) p.29. Reproduced with permission from Rugby Football Union.

**N. Fleming:** *Whole-body cryotherapy: what are the cold hard facts?* The Guardian: Health & wellbeing 24 July 2017, https://www.theguardian.com/lifeandstyle/2017/jul/24/whole-body-cryotherapy-what-are-cold-facts (The Guardian, 2017). Copyright Guardian News & Media Ltd 2019. Reproduced with permission.

**Sir E. Hillary:** quote (date unknown). Reproduced with permission from Director, E. Hillary IP.

**Men's Health:** *Get Andy Murray's Team GB diet plan*, Men's Health 7 March 2016 (Men's Health, 2016). Copyright menshealth.co.uk/Hearst Magazines UK. Reproduced with permission.

**Sport England:** *Youth Insights Pack*, August 2014 (Sport England, 2014). p.123. Reproduced with permission from Sport England.

**Sport England and the English Federation of Disability Sport:** *Mapping Disability: Engaging Disabled People: the guide*, 2016 (Sport England and the English Federation of Disability Sport, 2016). p.126. Reproduced with permission from Sport England.

**Sport England:** *Active Lives Adult Survey, November 16/17*, March 2018 (Sport England, 2018). p.128. Reproduced with permission from Sport England.

**Sport England:** *Active People Survey 6 Q2 (April 2011-April 2012)* (Sport England, 2012). p.129. Reproduced with permission from Sport England.

The publishers would like to thank the following for permission to use their photographs:

**Cover:** Tashi-Delek/iStock

**Artworks:** QBS Learning

Photos: **p4**: Alex Ferro/Jogos Rio 2016 via Getty Images; **p5**: Nancy Honey/Cultura RM/Alamy Foto Stock; **p12**: Icon Sportswire/Contributor/Getty Images; **p13**: Mitch Gunn/Shutterstock; **p15**: Nerthuz/Shutterstock; **p16** (T): Serena Taylor/Contributor/GettyImages; **p16** (B): RichardBakerRisk/Alamy Stock Photo; **p18** (L), **p71** (L): WENN Ltd/Alamy Foto Stock; **p18** (R): Jason O'Brien/Stringer/Getty Images; **p22**: Al Bello/Getty Images; **p23** (T): Jo Panuwat D/Shutterstock; **p23** (B): frentusha/iStockphoto; **p24** (T): Matt Frost/ITV/Rex/Shutterstock; **p24** (BL), **p51** (TL), **p52**: Sipa USA/REX/Shutterstock; **p24** (BR): Jarva Jar/Shutterstock; **p25** (TL): Gero Breloer/AP/Shutterstock; **p25** (R): Scott Barbour/Getty Images; **p25** (BL): Shaun Botterill/Getty Images; **p26**: Jacobs Stock Photography Ltd/DigitalVision/Getty Images; **p27**: Iakov Kalinin/123RF; **p28**: Larry French/NCAA Photos via Getty Images; **p31**: Valery Sharifulin\TASS via Getty Images; **p32**: Anton Starikov/Alamy Stock Photo; **p33** (T): Rashid Valitov/Shutterstock; **p33** (B): Golubovy/Shutterstock; **p34** (T): Michael Regan/Getty Images; **p34** (B): Ververidis Vasilis/Shutterstock; **p35** (T): sharky/Alamy Stock Photo; **p35** (BL), **p35** (BR): OSTILL is Franck Camhi/Shutterstock; **p39**: pterwort/Shutterstock; **p40** (T): MUNIR UZ ZAMAN/AFP/Getty Images; **p40** (M): INDRANIL MUKHERJEE/AFP/Getty Images; **p40** (B): Larry French/NCAA Photos via Getty Images; **p41**: Ian MacNicol/Getty Images; **p42** (TL): Gill/Topical Press Agency/Getty Images; **p42** (TR): bpk/Hubmann/ullstein bild via Getty Images; **p42** (BL): Jack Dawes/Daily Mail/Shutterstock; **p42** (BR): (c) DFKI; **p43**: Catherine Ivill - AMA/Getty Images; **p44** (TL): Ben Radford/Corbis via Getty Images; **p44** (TM):

Michael Regan - FIFA/FIFA via Getty Images; **p44** (B): By Permission of Hudl Sportscode; **p44** (TR): David Ramos/Getty Images; **p45**: David Madison/Getty Images; **p50**: Liderina/Shutterstock; **p51** (TM), **p53**: DAMIEN MEYER/AFP/Getty Images; **p51** (TR), **p54**: Laurence Griffiths/Getty Images; **p51** (BL), **p55**: Matthew Impey/Shutterstock; **p51** (M), **p56**: Eye Ubiquitous/REX/Shutterstock; **p51** (BM), **p57**: Matthias Schrader/AP/Shutterstock; **p51** (BR), **p58** (L): Aflo/Shutterstock; **p58** (R): Xinhua News Agency/REX/Shutterstock; **p61**: mimagephotography/Shutterstock; **p62**: PJF Military Collection/Alamy Stock Photo; **p63** (TR): JONATHAN NACKSTRAND/AFP/GettyImages; **p63** (ML): Tom Wang/Shutterstock; **p63** (BL): Dmitry Rukhlenko/Shutterstock; **p63** (BR): fizkes/Shutterstock; **p64**: Wavebreak Media/Alamy Stock Photo; **p65**: Di Studio/Shutterstock; **p67**: Halfpoint/Shutterstock; **p68** (L): Kjetil Kolbjornsrud/Shutterstock; **p68** (M): ESB Professional/Shutterstock; **p68** (R): WoodysPhotos/Shutterstock; **p71** (TR): Ian Hinchliffe/Alamy Stock Photo; **p71** (BR): Ian MacNicol/Getty Images; **p72**: Catalin Petolea/Shutterstock; **p73**: only_kim/Shutterstock; **p75**: vectorfusionart/Shutterstock; **p76** (L): New Africa/Shutterstock; **p76** (R): Sergey Nivens/Shutterstock; **p78** (T): Eddie Keogh For The FA/Shutterstock; **p78** (B): Ian Horrocks/Sunderland AFC via Getty Images; **p79**: Stu Forster/Getty Images; **p80**: Mike Harrington/Stone/Getty Images; **p81**: H. Mark Weidman Photography/Alamy Stock Photo; **p82**: UfaBizPhoto/Shutterstock; **p83** (T): New Africa/Shutterstock; **p83** (B): Igor Kovalchuk/Shutterstock; **p84** (T): 9dream studio/Shutterstock; **p84** (M): mahirart/Shutterstock; **p84** (B): exopixel/Shutterstock; **p85** (TL): Evlakhov Valeriy/Shutterstock; **p85** (TR): akepong srichaichana/Shutterstock; **p85** (BL): Kale Leaf/Shutterstock; **p85** (BR): Pineapple studio/Shutterstock; **p86** (TL): mahirart/Shutterstock; **p86** (TR): oksana2010/Shutterstock; **p86** (BL): donatas1205/Shutterstock; **p88**: Public Health England in association with the Welsh Government, Food Standards Scotland and the Food Standards Agency in Northern Ireland; **p89**: Clare Gainey/Alamy Stock Photo; **p91**: Jordan Mansfield/Getty Images for LTA; **p92** (TL): David Lee/Alamy Stock Photo; **p92** (TM): eye35.pix/Alamy Stock Photo; **p92** (TR): Helen Sessions/Alamy Stock Photo; **p92** (BL): Aleksandra Gigowska/Alamy Stock Photo; **p92** (BM): DenisMArt/Shutterstock; **p92** (BR): LMWH/Shutterstock; **p93**: Sarnia/Shutterstock; **p94**: AP/Shutterstock; **p95**: Jim Dyson/Redferns via Getty Images; **p98**: cheapbooks/Shutterstock; **p105**: LJM Photo/Getty Images; **p107** (TL): Dziurek/Shutterstock; **p107** (TM): Zoonar GmbH/Alamy Stock Photo; **p107** (TR): Foto Arena LTDA/Alamy Stock Photo; **p107** (BL): Hero Images/Getty Images; **p107** (BM): Serena Taylor/Newcastle United via Getty Images; **p108**: Sean Prior/Alamy Stock Photo; **p111** (L): Revierfoto/Action Press/Shutterstock; **p111** (R): Robbie Jay Barratt - AMA/Getty Images; **p112**: LOOK Die Bildagentur der Fotografen GmbH/Alamy Stock Photo; **p113** (T): Andrew Fosker/Shutterstock; **p113** (B): Vladimir Vasiltvich/Shutterstock; **p114**: sportpoint/Shutterstock; **p118**: Cultura Creative (RF)/Alamy Stock Photo; **p120**: Clint Hughes/Getty Images; **p122**: Tom Dulat/Getty Images for LTA; **p124**: pixelheadphoto digitalskillet/Shutterstock; **p125**: Golden Pixels LLC/Alamy Stock Photo; **p127**: Disability Images/Alamy Stock Photo; **p129**: Parmorama/Alamy Stock Photo; **p130**: Michael Turner/123RF; **p131** (TL): Ian MacNicol/Getty Images; **p131** (TR): The Fa/Shutterstock; **p131** (B): Richard Long/News Images/Shutterstock; **p132** (T): Image Source Plus/Alamy Stock Photo; **p132** (BL): yanik88/Shutterstock; **p132** (BM): Sergey Ryzhov/Shutterstock; **p132** (BR): tcsaba/Shutterstock; **p133**: DarioZg/Shutterstock; **p135**: LightField Studios/Shutterstock; **p136**: Naypong Studio/Shutterstock; **p138**: Sergio Azenha/Alamy Stock Photo; **p139**: Roddy Clark; **p139**: Roddy Clark; **p143**: wavebreakmedia/Shutterstock; **p150-p151**: Pavel L Photo and Video/Shutterstock; **p152** (T): drbimages/E+/Getty Images; **p152** (B): Dragon Images/Shutterstock; **p154**: David Freund/Photodisc/Getty Images; **p155**: sturti/iStockphoto

Thank you to James Helling for the index.

We have made every effort to trace and contact all copyright holders before publication, but if notified of any errors or omissions, the publisher will be happy to rectify these at the earliest opportunity.